Peter Christian's Recipes

Shirley Edes & Julia Philipson

Illustrated by Clinton Trefethen

T
&
R

To Karen Washburn, whose early
work in the kitchen created an inspired
basis for much of what has followed . . . .

Sixth   printing,   March   1987

Library of Congress Cataloging in Publication Data

Edes, Shirley, 1951-
Peter Christian's recipes.

Includes index.
1. Cookery.   I. Philipson, Julia, 1950-
II. Title.
TX715.E24 1983   641.5   83-374
ISBN 0-936988-09-6

© Shirley Edes, Julia Philipson, and Murray Washburn 1983
First published 1983 by Tompson & Rutter Inc
Grantham, New Hampshire 03753-0297
Printed in the United States of America

Contents

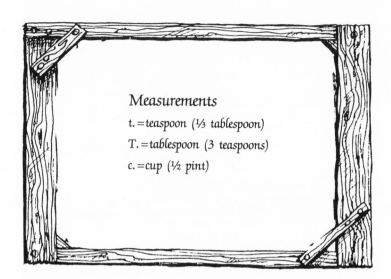

Measurements

t. = teaspoon (⅓ tablespoon)

T. = tablespoon (3 teaspoons)

c. = cup (½ pint)

Preface

". . . one of our readers has written to us most enthusiastically about the fine food you serve in your restaurant. Our correspondent particularly admired your Broccoli Quiche, and we wondered whether you would be willing to share the recipe with us . . ."

> Letter from Gourmet Magazine (recipe sent)

". . . one of our Bon Appetit readers admires your Mustard Sauce greatly and asked if you would be kind enough to supply the recipe . . ."

> Letter from Bon Appetit (recipe not sent*)

". . . and when we were in your New London restaurant in August, we enjoyed your Kahlua Brownie Chip pie; will you please send me . . ."

> Letter from a New York City visitor (recipe scribbled and sent)

". . . been coming here for years, but I won't mind waiting if you'll just aim me in the general direction of your Beef Stew recipe. I mean, you don't find stuff like that around . . ."

> Appreciative customer in corner booth in Hanover. (PC's recipe hastily reduced from gallons to cups and from cups to tablespoons; handwritten on PC stationery; happily handed to the patron.)

". . . thanks for giving me the Carob Mousse recipe. It was deelish! You know—have you ever though about writing a . . .?"

> Regular customer at the bar in New London.

". . . Well, let's do it! Let's write a proper cookbook!"

> *Determined conversation on the sunny porch of PC's, New London, among Shirley, Julia, Bea and myself. And so we have!*

My wife, Karen, and I founded the original "PC's" in Hanover in 1973. We planned it as a quiet family-and-friends effort, with carved wooden booths and tables, stoneware crocks and plates, and a deliberate emphasis on good food served in a setting that reflected "caring" by everyone—cooks, dishwashers, waiters, and all those who make a restaurant successful. The name derives not from eighteenth-century seafaring and shiphandling lore; rather, it is the first and middle names of our second son, an intellectual swashbuckler in his own right! There are now three PC's—Hanover, New London, and Keene (all in New Hampshire), and each has been planned with the same attention. We owe much to our staff, who share directly in the day-to-day management of their restaurants.

An anecdote about recipe replication—

Joni Mitchell (a musical idol of mine) wryly observed during a live concert, when implored by her fans to play an old favorite, that "painters create a masterpiece once, but musicians are asked to 'do it again'—and again and again!" The listener cherishes the notion that no musical hair will be out of place, and that the conditions that made this work so special in the original rendition will reproduce themselves concert after concert and time after time.

I can likely make the same observation about restaurant recipes. A certain special dish may have been savored at Peter Christian's with friends under delightful circumstances. But that dish is not the same again and again! All kinds of things made the food taste better: you were waited on, you did not have to do the cooking; no greasy pots and dishes reproached you from the sink; and the time, place, environment, conversation enhanced the meal, as well as just plain dining away from home!

For use in the home the restaurant recipe must be transposed from large, commercial quantities down to home cups and ounces—sometimes parting with a subtle something in the translation. Even the relative difference between home and commercial cookware and equipment can yield surprises.

Shirley Edes and Julia Philipson have spent hundreds of hours at their home kitchens, tinkering with ornery stoves, working with the same type of utensils and equipment you have in your own kitchens. They have pondered relative weights and measures, subjected friends and relatives to trial variation after trial variation (often with novel results), and washed the pots and dishes after each trial!

I think their results are magnificent, and I am confident you are going to enjoy reading, preparing, and digesting what lies ahead . . . even though your efforts may not absolutely replicate a special evening at PC's!

One last note: Shirley, Julia, and I are especially grateful to Bea Stedman for her patience and care in editing, typing (and retyping), and proofreading the galleys. She has also prepared the index, which is a helpful guide to this collection.

Murray Washburn

---

* Three popular recipes have never willingly left the restaurants, nor are they to be found within the pages of *Peter Christian's Recipes*. Withholding these is partly some good-natured cussedness on my part, and partly a marked deference and appreciation for their creators, to wit:

1. My mother, Barbara White, for **the** Mustard Sauce; a family treat from my youth, often discovered in a refrigerator crock, on my face, or between two pieces of bread piled with meats, cheeses, and lettuce.

2. Susan and Judy Dancik for PC's Carrot Cake, popular long before it became almost an American cult item. We thank them for sharing the recipe, and for baking and bringing the cakes into the restaurant when all we sported for equipment was a single-oven, crotchety electric range.

3. My Hawaiian friend, Marina, from Lanikai, Oahu, for PCO (Peter Christian's Own salad dressing).

Salads
and
Dressings

Mimosa Turkey Salad

1   Mix together in a large bowl
         4 c. diced cooked turkey
         2 c. diced celery
         ½ c. crushed pineapple, drained
         ½ c. coconut
         2 T. Rose's lime juice
         1 c. mayonnaise
         1 T. tarragon
         2 T. fresh chives.
         dash ginger.
2   Serve on shredded greens and garnish with coconut.

Serves 6 to 8

Pennsylvania Dutch Turkey Salad

1   Combine in bowl
         4 c. diced cooked turkey
         ¼ c. minced onion
         1 c. diced Lebanon bologna
         3 c. diced celery
         2 c. mayonnaise
         1 c. chopped dill pickles
         2 T. parsley flakes
         1 T. basil.
2   Serve on a bed of shredded greens.

Serves 6

Turkey, Avocado, and Bacon Salad

1   Mix together in a large bowl
        4 c. diced cooked turkey
        ¼ c. diced onion
        2 c. diced celery
        1 to 2 c. crumbled crisp bacon
        2 diced avocados, peeled
        2 c. mayonnaise
        ½ t. garlic salt
        1 T. lemon juice
        1 t. dill weed.
2   Serve on bed of shredded lettuce. (This also makes a good sand-
     wich spread.)

Serves 6 to 8

Apple Date Nut Salad

1   Mix until smooth with food processor or mixer
        1 lb. soft cream cheese
        1 c. mayonnaise
        2 T. maple syrup
        6 T. cream sherry
        ⅛ t. nutmeg.
2   Add to and mix well with
        12 c. (about 12) tart apples, cored, chopped, and
        unpeeled
        1 medium bunch celery, sliced
        1 lb. chopped dates.
3   Serve on leaf lettuce and garnish with toasted almonds, pecans,
     or peanuts.

Serves 10 to 12

4

Turkey Curry Salad

1   Mix together in a large bowl
            4 c. diced cooked turkey
            3 c. chopped celery
            3 c. diced unpeeled apples
            3 chopped hard boiled eggs
            1 c. raisins
            1 c. unsalted roasted peanuts or cashews
            1 T. Rose's lime juice
            1½ c. mayonnaise
            ¼ c. curry powder or to taste.
2   Serve on a bed of shredded lettuce.
3   Garnish with
            alfalfa sprouts
            extra nuts.

Serves 10 to 12

Dilled Chicken and Broccoli Salad

1   Mix in bowl
            4 c. diced cooked chicken
            ¼ c. minced onion
            1 bunch chopped cooked broccoli
            2 c. diced celery
            2 c. dill dressing.*
2   Serve on bed of shredded greens.
3   Garnish with alfalfa sprouts.

*See Dill Dressing recipe (page 12)
Serves 6

Mandarin Turkey Salad

1   Mix together in a large bowl
         4 c. diced cooked turkey
         ½ c. grated raw onion
         3 c. thinly sliced celery
         1 c. mayonnaise
         2 T. Rose's lime juice
         ½ t. salt or to taste
         2 T. tarragon.
2   Served on bed of shredded greens.
3   Garnish with
         mandarin oranges
         alfalfa sprouts
         toasted sliced almonds.

Serves 6 to 8

Ham and Artichoke Hearts Salad

1   Combine in a bowl
         1 8½-oz. can artichoke hearts, quartered and drained
         1 c. diced celery
         2 diced scallions
         3 c. diced cooked ham
         1 c. mayonnaise
         1 T. lemon juice
         1 T. wine vinegar
         1 t. basil
         1 t. oregano.
2   Serve on a bed of shredded greens and garnish with a lemon wedge and fresh parsley.

Serves 6 to 8.

Avocado Shrimp Salad

1   Mix together in a large bowl
        8 c. cooked shrimp
        2 c. finely chopped celery
        4 peeled and chopped avocados
        2 T. chives
        1 c. yogurt or sour cream
        1 c. mayonnaise
        2 T. lemon juice
        1 t. vinegar
        ½ t. salt
        ½ t. garlic power
        1 t. basil
        1 T. dill
        ¼ t. dry mustard.

2   Serve on a bed of shredded greens.

3   Garnish with
        alfalfa sprouts
        lemon slice.

Serves 8 to 10

Turkey, Apple, and Cashew Salad

1   Mix together in a large bowl

        4 c. diced cooked turkey

        4 c. tart unpeeled, cored, and diced apples

        2 c. chopped celery

        ¼ t. basil

        ⅛ t. summer savory

        ⅛ t. celery salt

        ⅛ t. nutmeg

        2 T. Rose's lime juice

        1 T. maple syrup (optional)

        dash of salt and pepper

        mayonnaise to desired consistency.

2   Serve on leaf lettuce and garnish generously with toasted cashews.

Serves 6 to 8

Marinated Mushrooms and Artichoke Hearts

1   Combine in a bowl

        1 lb. small cooked and cooled mushrooms

        1 8½-oz. can artichoke hearts, quartered

        vinaigrett dressing.*

2   Serve on a bed of mixed greens and garnish with a few alfalfa sprouts and fresh tomatoes.

*See Vinaigrette recipe (page 10)

Dressing for Fruit Salad

1   Mix well
  1 c. sour cream
  2½ c. mayonnaise
  ½ c. orange juice concentrate
  2 T. Rose's Lime Juice
  ¼ t. nutmeg.
2   Chill before using.

Makes about 4 cups

Blender Herb Hollandaise Sauce

1   Mix together in a blender on medium speed for 1 minute
  6 egg yolks (½ c.)
  ¼ c. lemon juice
  ¼ t. basil
  ¼ t. parsley
  ¼ t. dill.
2   Turn blender to high speed and add very slowly
  1 c. salted butter (½ lb.) melted.
3   Use immediately or chill to thicken for use in salads.

Makes about 2 cups

Vinaigrette Dressing

1   Whisk briskly in a bowl
                ½ c. mayonnaise
                ¼ c. vinegar
                ¼ c. oil
                2 t. garlic salt
                ½ t. thyme
                1 t. basil
                1 t. oregano.

Makes about 1 cup.

Tamari and Honey Dressing

1   Whisk briskly in a bowl
                1 c. salad oil
                ½ c. water
                ½ c. cider vinegar
                ½ c. tamari soy sauce
                2 T. honey
                2 t. lecithin granules
                ½ t. thyme
                ½ t. nutmeg
                1 t. oregano.

Makes about 2½ cups

Russian Dressing

1   Whisk until smooth
        1 c. mayonnaise
        ½ c. ketchup
        ⅓ c. chopped olives
        ⅓ c. chopped dill pickles
        1 t. horseradish
        1 t. Worcestershire sauce
        ½ t. salt
        ¼ t. pepper.

Makes about 2 cups.

Boursin Cheese

1   Beat until smooth
        8 oz. softened cream cheese
        1 T. lemon juice
        ½ t. garlic powder
        ½ t. basil
        ½ t. dill weed
        ¼ t. pepper
        ½ t. parsley
        ½ t. celery salt.

Makes about 1 cup

Dill Dressing

1   Whisk until smooth
            1 c. mayonnaise
            ½ c. buttermilk
            2 T. oil
            1½ T. dill
            ½ t. dry mustard
            2 t. onion salt
            3 T. cider vinegar.

Makes about 2 cups

Sandwiches

Peter's Father's Favorite

1   Layer on pumpernickel bread, in order,
           cream cheese horseradish spread*
           fresh spinach
           sliced roast beef
           thinly sliced onion
           sliced tomato.
2   Top with another slice of pumpernickel spread with cream
      cheese horseradish spread.*
3   Serve cold or heat in a microwave or hot oven.

*Cream Cheese Horseradish Spread
           *In a food processor or with an electric beater, mix softened cream cheese
           with horseradish to taste.*

Peter's Favorite Fantasy

1   Layer in order on the bread of your choice
           Boursin cheese*
           fresh spinach
           sliced turkey
           crisp bacon
           sliced tomatotes
           sliced roast beef
           Swiss cheese.
2   Cover with another slice of bread spread with mayonnaise.
3   Serve cold or heat in a microwave or hot oven.

*See Boursin Cheese recipe (page 11)

Peter's Blue Moon

1   Layer on pumpernickel bread, in order
        Blue cheese spread*
        fresh spinach
        sliced turkey
        sliced tomatoes
        crisp bacon.
2   Top with another slice of pumpernickel spread with blue cheese spread.
3   Serve cold or heat in a microwave or hot oven.

Blue Cheese Spread
        Mix yogurt with blue cheese until it is spreadable, but not runny.

Peter's Russian Mistress (open face)

1   Layer on bread of your choice, in order,
        fresh spinach
        sliced turkey
        sliced tomatoes
        crisp bacon
        Swiss cheese.
2   Broil until cheese melts.
3   Top with Russian dressing.*

*See Russian Dressing recipe (page 11)

Pete's Zaa

1   Heat 2 T. oil in a saucepan and sauté
           1 onion, diced
           2 green peppers, diced.
2   In another pan cook
           10 links sweet Italian sausage.
3   Drain grease from sausage and slice thin.
4   Add sausage to sautéed vegetables.
5   Mix in
           1 c. tomato sauce.
6   Season with
           2 t. oregano
           1½ t. basil
           ½ t. thyme.
7   Continue to cook over low heat for 10 minutes.
8   Remove from heat and add
           2 chopped fresh tomatoes.
9   Spread on Syrian Bread and top with
           Mozarella cheese.
10   Broil until cheese is bubbly.

Serve 4 to 6

Peter's Mother's Favorite

1   Layer on pumpernickel bread, in order,
        Peter Christian's mustard
        Cheddar cheese
        sliced ham
        sliced turkey
        sliced tomatoes
        Cheddar cheese.

2   Top with another slice of pumpernickel spread with mayonnaise.

3   Serve cold or heat in a microwave or hot oven.

Roast Beef with Sautéed Mushrooms and Onions (open face)

1   Layer on bread of your choice, in order,
        Dijon mustard
        sliced roast beef
        sautéed mushrooms and onions*
        Cheddar cheese.

2   Broil until cheese melts.

*Sautéed Mushrooms and Onions
        Sauté sliced mushrooms and diced onions in butter until tender. Season with a little garlic salt and thyme to taste.

Peter Christian's Pilgrim

1   Layer on bread of your choice, in order,
        mayonnaise
        sliced turkey
        apple stuffing.*
2   Top with another slice of bread spread with cranberry sauce.
3   Serve cold or heat in microwave or hot oven.

*See following recipe

Apple Stuffing

1   In a small frying pan melt
        3 T. butter.
2   Add finely chopped vegetables and sauté
        1 celery stalk
        ½ onion.
3   Toss lightly in a bowl
        6 diced slices of whole wheat bread
        1 diced apple
        1 t. poultry seasoning
        ½ t. salt
        ½ c. warm water.
4   Add sautéed vegetables.
5   Bake in a hot oven until top is crispy brown.

Holiday Hollandaise (open face)

1   Layer on bread of your choice, in order,
            mayonnaise
            fresh spinach
            sliced turkey or ham
            asparagus or broccoli (cooked and still hot).
2   Cover with Herb Hollandaise sauce* and serve immediately.

*See Blender Herb Hollandaise Sauce recipe (page 9)

New Orleans Muffeletta Pouch

1   Layer on Syrian bread, in order,
            Dijon mustard
            sliced turkey
            sliced salami
            Cheddar cheese
            ½ c. marinated vegetables.*
2   Serve cold or heat in a microwave or hot oven.

*Marinated Vegetables
    1   Drain and chop
            4 c. jardiniere (pickled mixed vegetables).
    2   Add to chopped vegetables
            ⅓ c. olive oil
            1 t. garlic
            1 T. oregano
            1 t. basil
            ½ t. thyme.
    3   Let sit for a couple of hours or overnight.

Serves 8

Ham, Egg Salad, and Spinach

1   Layer on bread of your choice, in order,
         sliced ham
         egg salad (with celery, chopped pickles and dill)
         fresh spinach.
2   Top with another slice of bread and spread with mayonnaise.

Baked Cheese and Olive

1   Cut 4 large sandwich rolls in half, spread each with melted
     butter and lightly sprinkle with
         basil
         garlic powder
         Parmesan cheese.
2   Bake at 350° for 10 to 15 minutes until golden brown.
3   Mix in a bowl
         6 c. Cheddar cheese
         ½ c. mayonnaise
         2 eggs
         1 c. chopped green olives*
         ½ t. basil
         2 T. fresh chives.
4   Divide among rolls and mound up in center.
5   Bake at 375° for 15 minutes.

Shrimp or green peppers or bacon can be used in place of olives

Turkey or Ham with Boursin Cheese

1   Layer on bread of your choice, in order,
          Boursin cheese*
          fresh spinach
          sliced turkey or ham
          sliced tomatoes.
2   Top with another slice of bread spread with Boursin cheese.*
3   Serve cold or heat in a microwave or hot oven.

*See Boursin Cheese recipe (page 11)

Asparagus Cordon Blue (open face)

1   Layer on bread of your choice, in order,
          Dijon mustard
          fresh spinach
          sliced ham
          asparagus, cooked and still hot
          Swiss cheese.
2   Broil until cheese is melted.

Hawaiian Sunset (open face)

1   Layer on bread of your choice, in order,
             sliced ham
             thinly sliced fresh pineapple
             Swiss cheese.
2   Broil until cheese is melted.

French Lieutenant's Woman

1   Mix together in a bowl
        1½ c. toasted pecan pieces
        4 c. diced turkey
        2 c. diced celery
        1½ c. mayonnaise
        2 t. basil
        1½ T. Rose's lime juice
        1 t. tarragon
        1 t. onion salt
        ¼ t. pepper.
2   Serve between pieces of hot French toast.

Gourmet Cheese, Tomato, and Sprouts

1   Layer on bread of your choice in order
        Boursin cheese*
        fresh spinach
        sliced tomatoes
        Swiss cheese
        sprouts.
2   Top with another slice of bread spread with Boursin cheese.*
3   Heat to melt cheese in a microwave or hot oven.

*See Boursin Cheese recipe (page 11)

Gourmet Tuna Melt

1   Layer in order on the bread of your choice
             Boursin cheese*
             fresh spinach
             tuna salad
             Swiss cheese.
2   Place under broiler to melt the cheese.

*See Boursin Cheese recipe (page 11)

Flying Saucer

1   On the bottom half of a hard roll, layer in order
             Boursin cheese*
             sliced roast beef
             sliced tomatoes
             crisp bacon
             Swiss cheese.
2   Cover sandwich with top of roll spread with Boursin cheese.*
3   Serve cold or heat in a microwave or hot oven.

*See Boursin Cheese recipe (page 11)

Soups

I can't honestly say that any soup I have ever made has come out the same twice. Soups have been born from leftovers, available vegetables, and too many chickens. And there are so many variables: the stocks, the herbs, and the dependability of your stove to simmer, or boil dry as soon as you answer the phone. But take heart, choose a recipe and rely on your taste buds to perfect your creations.

Don't be afraid to use your imagination to empty the refrigerator or use the garden surplus. But be sure to use quality products and herbs that are fresh. If any of the spices in the jars on your back shelf are beginning to resemble hay in either appearance or aroma, it's time to restock.

The body of your soup will be the broth. I have used a prepared base in these recipes, so don't fret about having to stand in front of a gurgling stock pot all day. However, if you do — God Bless you, and remember that you may need to add more salt than the recipes call for. Regardless of your stock, salt carefully and taste often.   S.E.

Chicken Victoria

1   In a soup kettle melt
        3 T. butter.
2   Dice and sauté in butter for 10 minutes
        1 celery stalk
        1 carrot
        1 medium onion
        1½ c. mushrooms.
3   Add to sautéed vegetables
        2 c. chicken broth
        ½ c. diced pimiento
        1½ c. diced cooked chicken.
4   Simmer for 15 minutes.
5   In a small bowl mix
        3 T. flour
        ¼ c. cold water.
6   Stir flour mixture into soup and continue to simmer until slightly thickened.
7   Season with
        1 T. tarragon
        1 t. basil
        ½ t. rosemary
        ½ t. thyme
        1 t. onion salt
        1 t. celery salt.
8   Continue to simmer over low heat, adding
        1½ c. light cream.

Serves 6

Beef Barley

1   Heat 4 T. oil in soup kettle. Brown for 15 minutes
        1 lb. diced stew beef, seasoned with
            ¼ t. pepper
            ½ t. minced garlic.

2   Add and simmer for 45 minutes
        ¾ c. pearl barley
        1 qt. beef stock.

3   Dice and add
        1 small onion
        1 celery stalk
        2 carrots
        1 c. mushrooms.

4   Continue to simmer.

5   When vegetables are tender season with
        1 t. basil
        1 t. thyme
        1 T. Worcestershire sauce
        2 t. onion salt
        ¼ c. Burgundy.

6   Simmer for 15 minutes more.

Serves 6

Canyon City

1   Heat 3 T. oil in soup kettle and sauté, diced,
    1 small onion
    1 celery stalk
    ½ green pepper
    3 cloves garlic.

2   Add and simmer for 20 minutes
    4 c. chicken broth
    1 lb. can stewed tomatoes
    1 lb. can corn
    1 lb. can shell beans
    20 green olives, quartered
    1 c. diced cooked chicken.

3   Season with
    1 t. celery salt
    4 t. chili powder
    2 t. cumin
    ½ t. cayenne.

4   Continue to simmer for 20 minutes.

5   When ready to serve, garnish each bowl with broken tortilla chips.

Serves 6

Eggplant Parmesan

1   Heat 2 T. oil in a heavy saucepan and brown
            ⅔ lb. hamburg.
2   In another pan sauté, diced,
            1 medium onion
            1 celery stalk
            2 garlic cloves
            3 c. eggplant.
3   When vegetables are tender add
            3 c. beef broth
            1 28-oz. can stewed tomatoes.
4   Simmer for ½ hour, then season with
            1 T. oregano
            1 T. basil
            ½ t. thyme.
5   Stir in hamburg and continue to simmer for 15 minutes.
6   When ready to serve, garnish with grated Parmesan cheese.

Serves 4 to 6

Beef Burgundy

1   Heat 2 T. oil in a heavy saucepan and brown 1 lb. stew meat
    cut in small pieces, seasoned with
    > ½ t. salt
    > ¼ t. pepper.
2   Add and simmer gently for 45 minutes
    > 2 c. beef broth
    > ½ c. Burgundy.
3   Add, chopped,
    > 2 carrots
    > 1 celery stalk
    > 1 medium onion
    > 1½ c. mushrooms.
4   Continue to simmer until vegetables are tender.
5   Season with
    > ½ c. Burgundy
    > 2 T. Worcestershire sauce
    > 2 T. parsley
    > ½ t. thyme
    > 1 T. basil.
6   Cook until flavors are well blended.
7   Add cooked egg noodles when ready to serve.

Serves 6

Chicken Curry

1   In 2 T. melted butter sauté, diced,
          1 small onion
          1 celery stalk.
2   Add
          4 c. chicken broth
          ⅓ c. uncooked long grain rice.
3   Cover and cook until rice is done.
4   Stir in
          1 c. milk
          1 c. light cream
          1½ c. diced cooked chicken
          ½ c. raisins
          2 T. curry powder
          salt to taste.
5   Simmer soup for 20 minutes.
6   When ready to serve garnish with
          1 chopped hard boiled egg
          chopped cashews or peanuts.

Serves 4 to 6

Broccoli Parmesan

1   Heat 2 T. butter in a soup kettle and sauté
          1 small onion, diced.
2   Add and cook, until broccoli is just tender,
          2 c. chicken broth
          1 bunch broccoli (diced stems and whole flowerets).

3   In a small bowl mix
          3 T. flour
          ¼ c. cold water.

4   Add flour mixture to soup, stirring until thickened.

5   Season with
          2 T. sherry
          ¾ c. Parmesan cheese
          2 t. basil
          2 t. onion salt
          ¼ t. nutmeg.

6   Continue to simmer for 20 minutes, adding
          1 c. milk
          1 c. light cream.

Serves 6

Cream of Celery with Almonds

1   Pour 2 c. chicken broth in a saucepan, adding, chopped,
          1 bunch of celery
          1 medium onion.

2   Cook until tender.

3   Puree vegetables and broth in a blender or food processor until smooth.

4   Return puree to kettle and simmer, adding
          2 c. milk
          2 T. sherry.

5   Season with
          1 t. celery salt
          ¼ t. nutmeg.

6   When ready to serve, garnish with sliced toasted almonds.

Serves 6

Chicken Divan

1   Melt in a heavy saucepan
        3 T. butter

2   Dice and sauté in butter
        1 medium onion
        2 celery stalks.

3   Add to sautéed vegetables
        2 c. chicken broth
        ½ bunch broccoli (diced stems and whole flowerets)
        1½ c. diced cooked chicken.

4   Simmer until broccoli is just tender.

5   In a small bowl mix
        ¼ c. cold water
        ¼ c. flour.

6   Stir flour mixture into soup, cooking until thickened.

7   Season with
        ¼ t. nutmeg
        1 t. rosemary
        2 t. onion salt.

8   Add
        1 c. light cream
        1 c. milk.

9   Simmer until flavors are well blended.

10   When ready to serve garnish with toasted slivered almonds.

Serves 4 to 6 ·

Dijon Beef

1   Heat 4 T. oil in a soup kettle; add and brown for 15 minutes

          1 lb. stew beef cut into small pieces

          1 t. granulated garlic

          ¼ t. pepper.

2   Add

          ½ c. dark beer

          1 qt. beef stock.

3   Simmer over low heat for 30 minutes.

4   Dice and add

          1 small onion

          1 celery stalk

          1 small turnip

          2 carrots

          1 c. cabbage.

5   Continue to simmer until vegetables are tender.

6   Season with

          1 t. thyme

          1 t. onion salt

          2 t. caraway seed

          4 t. Dijon mustard.

7   Cook soup for 20 minutes more.

8   Serve with pumpernickel croutons.*

*Cut pieces of pumpernickel bread in half. Cover each piece with a slice of Cheddar
cheese and broil in the oven until cheese is bubbly.

Serves 6

Ham Florentine

1   Heat 3 T. butter in a soup kettle and sauté
        1 medium diced onion.

2   Add
        ½ c. Chablis
        3 c. ham broth
        10 oz. frozen chopped spinach
        2½ c. diced ham.

3   Simmer for 20 minutes.

4   In a small bowl mix
        ¼ c. water
        5 T. flour.

5   Stir flour mixture into soup to thicken.

6   Continue to simmer, adding
        2½ c. grated mild Cheddar cheese.

7   When cheese has melted and is well blended, stir in
        2 c. light cream
        ½ t. tarragon
        salt to taste.

Serves 4

Corn Chowder

1 In a soup kettle melt
      3 T. butter.
2 Dice and sauté for 10 minutes
      1 medium onion
      1 celery stalk
      2 potatoes.
3 Add
      1 c. water.
4 Simmer until vegetables are tender.
5 Stir in
      2 1-lb. cans creamed corn
      2½ c. milk
      1 c. light cream.
6 Season with
      1 t. basil
      1 T. parsley
      ¼ t. pepper
      1 t. onion salt
      1 t. celery salt.
7 Continue to simmer for 20 minutes.

Serves 6

Broccoli Mushroom

1   Heat 2 T. butter in a soup kettle and sauté
        1 medium diced onion
        3 c. sliced mushrooms.
2   Add
        2 c. chicken broth
        1 bunch broccoli (diced stems and whole flowerets).
3   Simmer until broccoli is tender.
4   In a small bowl mix
        ¼ c. flour
        ¼ c. cold water
5   Add flour mixture to soup, stirring until thickened.
6   Season with
        ¼ t. nutmeg
        ¼ c. sherry
        salt and pepper to taste.
7   Continue to simmer for 15 minutes adding
        1½ c. milk
        1½ c. light cream.

Serves 6

Beef Stew

1   Heat 3 T. oil in heavy saucepan and brown
>   1 lb. stew meat, seasoned with
>>   1 t. garlic powder
>>   ¼ t. pepper.
2   Quickly stir in
>   3 T. flour.
3   Add
>   ½ bottle dark beer.
4   Simmer for 1 hour.
5   Add, coarsely chopped,
>   ¾ lb. carrots
>   3 medium potatoes
>   1 medium onion
>   1 small turnip
>   1 c. mushrooms.
6   Cover vegetables with water and cook until tender.
7   Season with
>   ½ t. thyme
>   1 T. basil
>   1 T. parsley
>   1 T. Worcestershire sauce
>   salt to taste.
8   Continue to simmer for 15 minutes.

Serves 6

Tomato Bisque

1   Melt 3 T. butter in a soup kettle and sauté, coarsely chopped,
         1 medium onion
         1 celery stalk.
2   Add to vegetables
         2 1-lb. cans stewed tomatoes
         1 t. basil
         ½ t. thyme
         1 t. oregano
         1 t. celery salt
         1 t. granulated garlic
         1 t. salt
         2 T. Burgundy.
3   Simmer for 20 minutes.
4   Remove from heat and puree mixture in a blender or food
     processor, adding
         1 c. light cream.
5   Garnish with
         dollop of sour cream
         fresh chives.

Serves 6

Broccoli Hollandaise

1 Cook in a soup kettle, until rice is tender,
   ½ c. rice
   1 qt. chicken stock.

2 Dice and add
   1 onion
   1 small bunch broccoli

3 Continue to simmer for 15 minutes.

4 Reduce heat and stir in briskly
   5 beaten eggs.

5 Continue cooking over low heat (be careful not to curdle by boiling) add
   2 c. milk
   1 c. cream
   7 T. lemon juice.

6 Season with
   1 t. tarragon
   2 T. onion salt.

7 Simmer until flavors are well blended.

Serves 8

Clam Chowder

1   In 2 T. melted butter dice and sauté until tender
        1 medium onion
        1 celery stalk.
2   Add
        3 medium diced potatoes
        juice from 3 6½-oz. cans of minced clams.
3   Simmer for 15 minutes.
4   In a small bowl mix
        2 T. flour
        ¼ c. cold water.
5   Stir flour mixture into vegetables simmering until thickened.
6   Season with
        1 T. parsley
        1 T. basil
        ¼ t. pepper
        1 t. onion salt
        ½ t. celery salt.
7   Add
        2 c. milk
        1 c. light cream
        3 cans of chopped clams, drained
        salt to taste.
8   Continue to simmer for 15 minutes.
9   Serve with a lemon wedge.

Serves 6 to 8

Dilled Asparagus Ham Chowder

1   Melt in a soup kettle
>3 T. butter.

2   Dice and sauté in butter for 10 minutes
>1 medium onion
>
>1 celery stalk
>
>1 potato
>
>8 asparagus spears.

3   Add
>1 c. diced ham
>
>2 c. water.

4   Simmer until vegetables are just tender.

5   In a small bowl mix:
>¼ c. water
>
>3 T. flour.

6   Add to soup, stirring until thickened.

7   Pour in
>2 c. milk
>
>1 c. light cream.

8   Continue cooking over low heat seasoning with
>1 T. onion salt
>
>¼ t. pepper
>
>1 t. basil
>
>1 T. dill weed.

9   Simmer 15 minutes until flavors are well blended.

Serves 6

Cream of Mushroom

1   Heat 3 T. butter in a soup kettle; dice and sauté
       1 medium onion
       1 celery stalk
       4 c. mushrooms.

2   When vegetables are tender, add
       ⅓ c. dry white wine
       2 c. chicken broth.

3   Simmer for 10 minutes.

4   In a small bowl mix
       ½ c. cold water
       ¼ c. flour.

5   Stir flour mixture into soup and cook until thickened.

6   Season with
       1 t. granulated garlic
       1 t. thyme
       1 t. basil
       ¼ t. pepper
       2 t. onion salt
       1 t. salt.

7   Continue to cook over low heat for 15 minutes, adding
       ¼ c. sherry
       2 c. light cream.

Serves 6

French Onion Soup

1.   In 2 T. melted butter, sauté until transparent
          6 medium onions, thinly sliced.
2.   Add
          3 T. sherry.
3.   Continue to simmer for 15 minutes.
4.   Cover with
          4 c. beef broth.
5.   Continue to cook over low heat for 20 minutes, seasoning with
          1 T. soy sauce
          1½ T. basil
          ½ t. thyme
          salt to taste.
6.   When ready to serve, put in each bowl of soup
          1 French bread crouton*
          1 thick slice of Swiss cheese.
7.   Place under broiler until cheese bubbles.

*Brush 1 piece of French bread with melted butter and sprinkle with Parmesan cheese, garlic powder, and basil. Toast in 350° oven for 15 minutes, until crisp and lightly brown.

Serves 6

Fish Chowder

1   In a heavy soup kettle simmer
        1 12-oz. can clam broth
        2 diced potatoes
        2 diced celery stalks
        1 diced onion
        1 lb. white fish fillets, chopped.

2   When vegetables are tender, season with
        1 t. basil
        1 T. parsely flakes
        1½ t. onion salt
        1 t. celery salt
        ¼ t. pepper.

3   In another small pan, melt
        ¼ c. butter.

4   Stir in
        ¼ c. flour.

5   Cook over low heat 5 minutes, stirring constantly.

6   Stir roux into vegetables and simmer until thickened.

7   Add
        1 c. milk
        1 c. light cream.

8   Simmer another 10 minutes.

9   When ready to serve, garnish with a lemon wedge.

Serves 4 to 6

Italian Sausage and Bean

1   In a heavy soup kettle cook until done
        4 hot Italian sausages
        4 sweet Italian sausages.

2   Remove sausages from the pan and pour off all but 2 to 3 T. drippings. Dice and sauté in drippings
        2 cloves garlic
        1 medium onion
        ½ green pepper
        1 celery stalk.

3   Slice sausages into thin pieces and return to pan.

4   Simmer and add
        1 qt. beef stock
        1 lb. can stewed tomatoes
        1 lb. can shell or fava beans.

5   Season with
        2 T. parsely
        2 T. basil
        1 T. oregano
        ½ t. thyme.

6   Continue to simmer for 20 minutes more.

Serves 6

Lentil Soup

1   Soak overnight in cold water
           1 lb. lentils.

2   Cook lentils for 1 hour in
           7 c. water
           2 bay leaves.

3   Meanwhile, in another pan, sauté
           ¼ lb. diced bacon.

4   Remove bacon from pan. Dice and sauté in remaining fat
           1 medium onion
           1 celery stalk
           2 carrots.

6   Add sautéed vegetables to lentils.

7   Continue to cook lentils for another ½ hour adding
           bacon
           1 lb. can stewed tomatoes.

8   Season with
           2 t. basil
           ½ t. thyme
           1 T. onion salt
           1 T. vegetable salt
           ¼ t. pepper
           2 T. soy sauce.

9   Simmer on low heat for 20 minutes.

Serves 6

Minestrone

1   Heat 3 T. oil in a soup kettle; add and brown
    ¾ lb. stew beef, diced and seasoned with
      2 cloves garlic, minced
      ¼ t. pepper.

2   Add
    6 c. water.

3   Simmer for 45 minutes.

4   Add chopped
    ½ green pepper
    1 small onion
    1 carrot
    1 celery stalk.

5   Continue to simmer until vegetables are tender.

6   Add
    1 c. uncooked macaroni
    1 lb. can stewed tomatoes
    1 6-oz. can tomato paste
    1 c. cooked chick peas
    1 c. cooked kidney beans
    1 c. Italian or green beans.

7   Continue to simmer until macaroni is done, seasoning with
    1 t. thyme
    1 T. parsley
    1 T. oregano
    1 t. basil
    1 to 2 T. onion salt
    1 T. celery salt.

8   Garnish with grated Parmesan cheese.

Serves 8

Cream of Spinach

1   In a soup kettle simmer
         2 c. chicken broth
         1 medium onion, diced
         1 T. lemon juice
         1 10-oz. package frozen chopped spinach.
2   After cooking for 15 minutes add
         ½ t. tarragon
         ¼ t. nutmeg.
3   Remove pan from heat and puree soup in blender or food
     processor until smooth, adding
         4 oz. cream cheese.
4   Return puree to stove and add
         ½ c. plain yogurt
         salt to taste.
5   Cook just until hot, being careful not to boil or it will curdle.
6   Garnish with lemon wedges.

Serves 4

Pennsylvania Dutch
Chicken Corn Chowder

1   Melt 3 T. butter in a heavy kettle. Dice and sauté
         1 small onion
         1 celery stalk
         1 large potato.

2   Add and simmer until vegetables are tender
         1 c. water
         1 c. diced cooked chicken
         ½ c. diced smoked sausage or Lebanon bologna.

3   Add and continue to simmer gently
         1 lb. can creamed corn
         2 c. milk
         1 c. light cream.

4   Season with
         1 t. onion salt
         1 t. parsley
         1 t. basil.

5   Simmer until herbs are well blended.

Serves 6

Mushroom Wild Rice

1   In a saucepan cook until tender
       ¾ c. rice and wild rice mixture
       2 c. water.

2   Heat 3 T. butter in another pan, dice and sauté
       1 medium onion
       2 carrots
       1 celery stalk
       ½ green pepper
       4 c. mushrooms.

3   When vegetables are tender, add
       6 c. beef broth
       cooked rice and wild rice mixture.

4   Continue to simmer for 10 minutes seasoning with
       1 T. parsley
       1 T. basil
       1 t. granulated garlic
       ½ t. thyme.

Serves 6

Cream of Potato with Dill

1   Cook in soup kettle, until vegetables are tender
       6 quartered medium potatoes
       2 chopped celery stalks
       1 quartered medium onion
       2 c. chicken broth
       1 t. salt.

2   Remove from stove and puree mixture in a blender or food processor until smooth.

3   Return to kettle and cook gently for 15 minutes with

    1 T. basil
    2 T. dill weed
    1 c. light cream
    dash of pepper.

4   Serve with a dollop of sour cream and fresh chopped chives.

This soup is also excellent cold.

Serves 4 to 6

Tomato Zucchini

1   In 3 T. melted butter sauté until tender

    3 small zucchini, sliced
    1 small onion, diced
    ½ green pepper, diced
    2 celery stalks, diced
    2 garlic cloves, minced.

2   Add and simmer for ½ hour

    4 c. chicken broth
    1 lb. 12 oz. can stewed tomatoes.

3   Season with

    1 T. basil
    1 T. oregano
    ½ t. thyme
    ¼ t. pepper
    salt to taste.

4   Continue to simmer until flavors are blended.

Serves 6

Oriental Pork

1   Heat 3 T. oil in a heavy soup kettle; add and brown for 10 minutes
>
> 1 lb. diced pork
>
> 2 cloves minced garlic
>
> ½ t. ginger.

2   Add to pork mixture
>
> 4 c. water
>
> 3 T. Tamari soy sauce

3   Simmer for 20 minutes.

4   Add and cook until tender
>
> 1 medium diced onion
>
> 1 c. sliced mushrooms
>
> 1 celery stalk (sliced diagonally)
>
> 1 8-oz. can bamboo shoots
>
> 1 8-oz. can sliced water chestnuts.

6   Season with
>
> ⅓ c. oyster sauce
>
> 1 T. sesame oil.

7   Simmer for 10 more minutes, adding
>
> ½ 6-oz. package frozen pea pods.

Serves 6

Split Pea with Ham

1   Soak overnight in cold water
          1 lb. split green peas.

2   Cook peas for 1 hour over low heat in
          6 c. ham broth.

3   Dice and add
          1 medium onion
          2 carrots
          1 c. ham.

4   Continue to simmer for 30 minutes, seasoning with
          ¼ t. basil
          ½ t. thyme
          ¼ t. pepper
          salt if necessary.

5   When ready to serve, stir in
          ½ c. light cream
          top with buttered, toasted croutons.

Serves 6

Vegetable

1   In a large soup kettle simmer for 1 hour
             6 c. water
             1 c. corn
             1 c. green beans
             1 c. chopped green cabbage
             ½ diced green pepper
             1 stalk diced celery
             1 diced potato
             1 chopped onion
             1 can (1 lb. 12 oz.) stewed tomatoes.
2   Season with
             2 t. garlic salt
             2 t. onion salt
             ½ t. celery salt
             1 T. parsley
             ¼ t. thyme
             2 t. basil
             1 T. oregano.
3   Continue to simmer until flavors are blended.

Serves 6

Sherry Chicken Chowder

1   In a large soup kettle melt
     3 T. butter.

2   Dice and sauté in butter for 10 minutes
     1 c. mushrooms
     1 medium onion
     1 celery stalk
     1 carrot.

3   Add to vegetables
     2 c. chicken broth
     ½ c. sherry.

4   Simmer until vegetables are tender.

5   In a small bowl mix
     3 T. flour
     ¼ c. cold water.

6   Stir flour mixture into vegetables and simmer until thickened, stirring often.

7   Add to soup
     1 c. cooked barley
     1½ c. diced cooked chicken.

8   Season with
     1 T. parsley
     ½ t. thyme
     1 t. rosemary
     1 t. celery salt
     1 t. onion salt.

9   Continue to cook over low heat for 15 minutes adding
     2 c. light cream
     1 T. sherry.

Serves 6

Vermont Cheddar

1   Heat 3 T. butter in a soup kettle; add and sauté for 5 minutes
        1 small onion, minced.

2   Stirring constantly, add
        ¼ c. flour
        3 c. milk.

3   Cook over low heat until thickened.

4   Grate and add to soup
        1 lb. Vermont Cheddar cheese.

5   Season with
        1 T. Worcestershire sauce
        ⅓ c. dry white wine
        1 t. onion salt
        ½ t. granulated garlic
        ½ t. dry mustard
        ½ t. dill weed.

9   Simmer over very low heat for 15 minutes.

10   Add
        1 c. light cream.

Serves 6

Gazpacho

1   Puree in a blender or food processor
    2 tomatoes.

2   Mix in a bowl with
    2 c. V-8 juice.

3   Finely dice
    1 small onion
    1 cucumber, peeled and seeded
    1 green pepper
    1 celery stalk
    1 small zucchini
    1 small carrot.

4   Add vegetables to tomato mixture, then season with
    2 T. lemon juice
    1 t. basil
    1 t. oregano
    ½ t. thyme
    1 t. granulated garlic
    2 t. Worcestershire sauce
    1 t. salt
    Tabasco to taste.

5   Chill for several hours.

6   When ready to serve, garnish with a lemon wedge and fresh chopped parsley.

Serves 6

Chilled Blueberry Soup

1   Strain, reserving juice,
          1 15-oz. can blueberries.
2   In ⅓ c. of the juice dissolve
          1½ t. plain gelatin.
3   Heat gelatin mixture in small saucepan to boiling point.
4   Remove from heat.
5   Mix in a bowl
          1 c. plain yogurt
          ½ c. orange juice
          ⅓ c. heavy cream
          1½ T. honey
          ¼ t. cinnamon.
6   Add
          gelatin mixture
          remaining blueberries and juice.
7   Chill until thickened.
8   Serve with a dash of nutmeg.

Serves 4

Chilled Avocado and Zucchini Soup

1   Puree in a food processor or blender until smooth
        2 ripe avocados, peeled and diced
        2 c. cooked, cooled zucchini
        ¼ c. chopped scallion tops or fresh chives
        3 T. lemon juice
        2½ c. heavy cream
        1 t. dill
        ¼ t. basil
        ¼ t. garlic powder
        ½ t. salt
        dash of pepper.

2   Pour into a bowl and stir in
        4 c. cold chicken broth.

3   Chill until very cold and serve with a thin slice of lemon and fresh chives.

Serves 6 to 8

Iced Melon Soup

1   Puree in blender or food processor until smooth
        1 c. orange juice
        fruit from a very ripe cantaloupe
        3 T. melon liquor.
2   Add to fruit puree
        2 c. diced honeydew (also very ripe).
3   Chill for at least 1 hour.
4   When ready to serve, garnish with fresh mint.

Serves 4

Chilled Peach and Almond

1   In a blender or food processor puree
        2 c. orange juice
        2 to 3 T. Amaretto (or peach brandy)
        3 peaches (pitted, but not peeled).
2   Add to this puree
        1 diced peach.
3   Chill well.
4   When ready to serve, garnish with toasted sliced almonds.

Serves 4

Hot Dishes

Something that can be put into a crepe, can be put into a turnover or under puff pastry or in a patty shell. Ham could be turkey, or broccoli could be asparagus, if it sounds good to you or if you have one and not the other. I have put together a reasonable representation of sauces and fillings, and I hope you will experiment with different combinations. I think at one time or another I have put nearly everything you can think of together one way or another. Common sense and your own taste should guide you. To substitute scallions for chives is fine, but using strong onions is going too far. Shrimp for crab meat would be great, but tuna might be dreadful. One note on the sauces—I make them pretty thick most of the time, for the dishes are reheated in a microwave and the sauces can get very watery. If a sauce seems too thick to you, just add more milk or cream for the consistency you prefer. All of the casseroles and hot dishes can be made ahead and even frozen and heated later. Cover with plastic (use toothpicks to keep the plastic off the sauce) to heat in the microwave so the food doesn't dry out, or use foil for a conventional oven.   J.P.

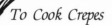

To Cook Crepes

1   Lightly oil an 8-inch crepe pan and heat over medium flame until a drop of water beads and disappears immediately on surface.
2   Quickly pour a scant ¼ c. of batter into pan, turning the pan in a circular motion quickly to cover the bottom.
3   Cook until crepe loses wet appearance and is lightly browned on underside.
4   Loosen sides of crepe with a rubber spatula, then turn and brown lightly on the other side.
5   Remove from pan onto paper towels and cool until ready to fill.

Dilled Shrimp and Broccoli Crepes

1   Cook and cool Parmesan or Whole Wheat Crepes (pages 67 and 69).

Dill Havarti Sauce

2   Melt in saucepan
>1 c. butter.

3   Stir in until smooth
>1 c. flour.

4   Stir in
>4½ c. light cream or milk
>
>1 t. salt
>
>1 t. dill
>
>½ t. basil.

5   Cook over low heat, stirring frequently until thick.

6   Stir in and cook until cheese melts
>2 c. Dill Havarti cheese (if unavailable, use Monterey Jack cheese and increase dill to 1 T.)

Filling

7   Mix in a large bowl
>8 c. cooked broccoli
>
>8 c. cooked shrimp
>
>1 c. chopped scallions (with green tops)
>
>half of cheese sauce.

8   Divide filling evenly among crepes. Roll up.

9   Top evenly with remaining cheese sauce and sprinkle with dill.

10   Bake at 350° 15 minutes to heat through. Serve 2 per person.

Makes 28 crepes

Ham Florentine Crepes

1   Cook and cool Parmesan or Whole Wheat crepes (pages 67 and 69).

2   In frying pan melt
        2 T. butter.

3   Add and sauté until tender, but still a little crisp,
        3 c. sliced celery
        ½ to 1 c. chopped onion.

4   Combine celery and onion in a bowl with
        8 c. cubed cooked ham
        2 c. cooked and well drained chopped spinach (approximately 2 boxes frozen).

Florentine Sauce

5   In a saucepan melt
        1 c. butter.

6   Add and stir in until smooth
        1 c. flour.

7   Stir in until smooth, then cook over low heat, stirring frequently, until thick,
        4½ c. light cream or milk
        1 t. salt
        1 t. celery salt
        ¼ t. garlic salt
        3 T. lemon juice
        1 t. dill
        ½ t. basil.

8   When sauce is thick, stir in until well mixed (or puree all in blender for a smooth sauce)
        1 c. cooked, well drained spinach (1 box frozen).

9   Add half of sauce to ham mixture.

10   Divide filling evenly among crepes and roll up.

11   Cover evenly with remaining sauce and bake at 350° 10 to 15 minutes to heat through. Serve 2 or 3 per person.

This is also good with cooked broccoli or asparagus.

Makes 28 crepes

Parmesan Crepes

1   Mix in blender until smooth

      4 eggs

      1 c. milk

      1 c. water

      4 T. oil

      ¾ c. white flour

      ¼ c. whole wheat flour

      ¼ c. Parmesan cheese

      ½ t. salt

      ½ t. basil

      ½ t. parsley

      ½ t. dill (if for seafood).

2   Let batter stand for 30 minutes before cooking.

Turkey and Mushroom Crepes

1   Cook and cool Parmesan or Whole Wheat crepes (pages 67 and
    69).
2   In a large frying pan melt
        2 T. butter.
3   Add, cover and cook on medium high heat until mushrooms
    are tender
        8 c. sliced mushrooms
        ¼ c. sherry.
4   Drain mushrooms reserving juice.
5   In same frying pan melt
        2 T. butter.
6   Add and sauté until tender, but still rather crisp,
        1 or 2 c. celery.
7   Combine mushrooms and celery in a large bowl with
        8 c. cubed cooked turkey or chicken
        1 or 2 c. chopped scallions or red onions.

Mushroom Sauce

8   In a saucepan melt
        1 c. butter
9   Add and stir in until smooth
        1 c. flour.
10 Add light cream or milk to reserved mushroom juice to make
    4 c. Add to butter and flour mixture and stir until smooth.
11 Add and cook over low heat until thick, stirring frequently,
        2 chicken boullion cubes
        ½ t. thyme
        1 t. basil
        1 t. salt or to taste
        dash of pepper
        ½ c. sherry.

12   Stir half of sauce into turkey and mushroom mixture.

13   Divide filling evenly among crepes and roll up.

14   Top evenly with remaining sauce and sprinkle with parsley.

15   Bake at 350° 10 to 15 minutes to heat through. Serve 2 or 3 per person.

Makes 28 crepes

Whole Wheat Crepes

1   Mix in blender until smooth
   4 eggs
   1 c. milk
   ¾ c. water
   4 T. melted butter or oil
   ½ c. whole wheat flour
   ½ c. white flour
   ½ t. salt.

2   Let batter stand for 30 minutes before cooking.

Makes 28 crepes.

Turkey and Broccoli Turnovers

1   Melt in a small fry pan
        1 T. butter.

2   Add and sauté until just tender
        ½ c. celery
        ½ c. scallions or sweet onions.

3   Mix well in a bowl with
        3 c. diced cooked turkey or chicken
        2 c. cooked broccoli, cut in small pieces (1 small bunch).

Cheddar Sauce

4   Melt in a saucepan
        ½ c. butter.

5   Stir in
        ½ c. flour.

6   Add and stir in until smooth
        3 c. light cream or milk
        1 t. salt
        ½ t. celery salt
        ½ t. basil.

7   Cook until thick, stirring often over low heat.

8   Add and stir over medium heat until melted
        2 c. Cheddar cheese.

9   Add 1 c. sauce to turkey and broccoli. Keep remaining sauce warm.

10 Cut puff pastry into 6 pieces, 5"x8", and divide filling evenly among pieces. Fold around filling and crimp edges with a fork. Pierce top with fork to release steam.

11 Bake at 425° 15 to 20 minutes until browned and puffed.

12 Serve immediately with remaining sauce.

Serves 6

Stuffed Potato

1 Bake at 350° 1 hour or until tender
   6 large baking potatoes.
2 Slice off top quarter of potato lengthwise and scoop out insides.
3 Mash potato with
   ¼ c. butter
   ¼ or ½ c. cream
   ¼ c. sour cream
   salt and pepper to taste
   ½ t. celery salt.
4 Stir in until well distributed
   1 c. cubed cooked turkey or chicken
   1 c. cubed Cheddar or Swiss cheese
   ¼ c. Lebanon bologna or cooked bacon
   ¼ c. chopped scallions or chives
   2 T. chopped fresh parsley.
5 Stuff potato and bake at 350° for 15 minutes to heat through.
6 Serve hot with
   sour cream
   chives
   crumbled bacon.

Serves 6

Stuffed Eggplant

1   Cut in half lengthwise, scoop out inside leaving a ½" shell, and steam 10 minutes until tender
        4 medium 6" to 8" eggplants.

2   Chop scooped out eggplant to measure 3 c. and set aside (discard the rest).

3   In a large frying pan or soup kettle heat
        2 T. olive oil.

4   Add and brown
        2 lb. sliced sweet Italian sausage.

5   Add and cook until just tender (10 to 15 minutes)
        2 c. chopped onions
        2 c. chopped green peppers
        3 cloves garlic, minced.

6   Add and cook 10 minutes
        reserved 3 c. eggplant.

7   Stir in and simmer on medium heat 20 to 30 minutes, stirring often until liquid is mostly absorbed,
        4 c. chopped fresh tomatoes
        ¼ c. red wine
        2 t. basil
        2 t. oregano
        ½ to 1 t. salt
        pepper to taste.

8   Stir in just enough to hold mixture together
        1 to 2 c. dry seasoned bread crumbs.

9   Mound filling into steamed eggplant shells and cover with
        1 to 2 c. grated Swiss or Cheddar cheese

10 Bake at 375° 15 minutes to melt cheese and heat through.

Serves 8

Salmon Turnovers

1   Drain and bone, saving liquid,
        1 16-oz. can salmon.
2   Mix salmon with
        ¼ c. chopped scallions
        1 egg
        ½ t. dill
        1 t. lemon juice
        ¼ t. garlic salt
        dash pepper.
3   Thaw puff pastry and cut in pieces, roughly 5″x8″. Cut any excess into leaf shapes to decorate tops of turnovers.
4   In each rectangle of dough place 1″ from edge
        a 2″ square ¼″ thick slice of cream cheese
        ¼ of salmon mixture.
5   Wrap pastry around filling and crimp with a fork. Decorate with reserved leaves, if desired. (Wet one side of pastry and press on so it will stick).
6   Bake at 400° 15 to 20 minutes until pastry is puffed and golden brown.
7   Serve with ¼ c. dill sauce (see below) and a sprig of fresh parsley or dill.

Dill Sauce

8   Puree in blender and chill until ready to use
        8 oz. cream cheese
        ⅓ c. salmon juice
        2 T. buttermilk or yogurt
        1 t. lemon juice
        ¼ t. basil
        ¼ t. garlic salt
        ½ t. dill.

Serves 4

PC's Quiche

Pastry

1   In a mixing bowl combine
    1¼ c. flour
    ¼ c. whole wheat flour
    ½ t. salt.

2   With a pastry blender cut in until mixture resembles oatmeal
    ½ c. butter.

3   In a measuring cup whisk together
    1 egg
    ½ c. ice water.

4   Add water to flour mixture until you can make a ball out of the dough that holds together well.

5   Roll out on a floured surface and fit into a 10″ quiche pan or pie plate.

Custard

6   Combine well in a bowl using a whisk
    4 eggs
    2 c. light cream (or 1 c. light and 1 c. heavy)
    ¼ c. sherry
    dash pepper
    dash nutmeg
    dash cayenne pepper.

Cheese

7   Have on hand
    4 to 6 c. grated cheese. (We use a combination of Swiss Gruyère, Dill Havarti, and Cheddar. At least half of the combination should be Swiss.)

Assemble

8   Sprinkle in bottom of crust

         1 c. grated cheese

         ½ c. chopped scallions or cooked and cooled chopped onions.

9   Cover cheese and onions with

         1 to 2 c. cooked and cooled vegetables or meat of your choice.

10   Cover meat or vegetables with remaining cheese.

11   Pour custard over cheese within ¼″ of top of crust.

12   Bake at 425° for 10 minutes. (If you use a 2-piece quiche pan, put a round pizza pan under the quiche pan for any drips.)

13   Reduce heat to 325° and bake another 45 to 50 minutes until golden brown and slightly puffed on the edges.

14   Let quiche stand 15 to 20 minutes to set before cutting.

Serves 8 to 10

Chicken Breasts with Shrimp

1   With a meat mallet, pound between plastic wrap to an even thickness and set aside

        6 boned skinned chicken breasts.

2   In a bowl combine

        4 c. cooked small shrimp

        2 c. chopped scallions with green tops.

Mornay Sauce

3   In a saucepan melt

        ½ c. butter.

4   Stir in until smooth

        ½ c. flour.

5   Stir in until smooth and cook over low heat, stirring frequently,

        2½ c. light cream or milk

        1 chicken bouillion cube

        ½ t. salt or to taste

        1 t. dill

        ¼ t. basil.

6   When sauce is thick, add and stir over medium heat until cheese melts

        ½ c. dry white wine

        2 c. grated Swiss cheese.

7   Stir half of Mornay cheese sauce into shrimp mixture.

8   Divide shrimp evenly among chicken breasts and roll chicken around filling. Place seam side down in individual casserole dishes or in a baking dish all together.

9   Cover evenly with remaining cheese sauce and bake at 375° 20 to 25 minutes until chicken is cooked through.

This is also good with 1 to 2 c. of mushrooms or cooked broccoli or asparagus added.

Serves 6

Chicken Breasts
with Broccoli and Hollandaise Sauce

1   With a meat mallet, pound between plastic wrap to an even thickness and set aside
      6 boned skinned chicken breasts.

2   Steam until just barely tender
      2 to 3 c. broccoli (1 bunch) cut in 3″ pieces.

3   Sprinkle inside of chicken lightly with dill, then place ⅓ to ½ c. of cooked broccoli in center and roll chicken around it. Place seam side down in individual casserole dishes or all together in a baking pan.

4   Over each breast, spoon
      1 T. dry white wine.

5   Cover and bake at 350° 20 to 25 minutes or until chicken is just done.

6   While chicken is baking, prepare ½ recipe of Blender Herb Hollandaise sauce.*

7   Remove chicken from oven and cover immediately with Hollandaise sauce. Serve at once. Garnish with fresh parsley or dill and a slice of lemon.

*See Blender Herb Hollandaise Sauce recipe (page 9)
Serves 6

Chicken Breasts with Asparagus

1   With a meat mallet, pound between plastic wrap to an even thickness and set aside
         6 boned and skinned chicken breasts.

2   Steam until tender
         5 c. fresh asparagus cut in 3" pieces.

3   Combine asparagus in a bowl with
         1 c. chopped scallions.

Velouté Sauce

4   In a saucepan, melt
         ½ c. butter.

5   Stir in until smooth
         ½ c. flour.

6   Stir in and cook over low heat until thick and smooth
         1½ c. chicken broth
         ½ c. dry white wine.

7   In a small bowl combine well, then stir quickly into sauce
         1 c. heavy cream
         1 egg yolk
         ¼ c. Parmesan cheese.

8   Continue to cook and stir until sauce is heated through, but don't let it boil or it will curdle.

9   Season sauce with:
         ½ t. basil or summer savory
         celery salt to taste
         salt and pepper.

10   Stir half of sauce into asparagus.

11   Divide asparagus mixture evenly among chicken breasts and roll chicken around filling. Place seam side down in individual casserole dishes or all together in a flat baking dish.

12   Cover evenly with remaining sauce and bake at 375° 20 to 25 minutes until chicken is cooked through.

This is also good with cooked broccoli.

Serves 6

Celery Almond Chicken Breasts

1 In a flat pan, toast at 350° for 15 minutes or until light brown
   1½ c. slivered almonds.

2 With a meat mallet, pound between plastic wrap to an even thickness and set aside
   6 chicken breasts, boned and skinned.

3 In a frying pan, melt
   2 T. butter.

4 Add and sauté until tender, but still a little crisp,
   2 c. chopped celery (4 stalks)
   2 c. chopped onions (2 medium).

5 Combine celery and onion in a bowl with
   1 c. toasted almonds.

6 Mix ½ of Sherry Cheddar Sauce (see below) into celery almond mixture.

7 Divide celery almond mixture evenly among chicken breasts and roll chicken around filling. Place seam side down in individual casserole dishes or all together in a baking dish.

8 Cover evenly with remaining cheese sauce and bake at 375° 20 to 25 minutes until chicken is cooked through. Sprinkle with remaining almonds to serve.

Sherry Cheddar Sauce

9 In a saucepan melt
   ½ c. butter.

10 Stir in until smooth
   ½ c. flour.

11	Stir in and cook over low heat, stirring frequently until smooth and thick

>	2½ c. light cream or milk
>	1 chicken boullion cube
>	½ t. basil
>	½ t. celery salt
>	¼ t. thyme.

12	When sauce is thick, stir in over medium heat until cheese melts

>	1½ c. sharp Cheddar cheese
>	½ c. sherry.

Serves 6

Eggplant Florentine

1   Cut in ½″ slices
        1 large eggplant.
2   Brush both sides of eggplant with melted butter and arrange on
    baking sheet and sprinkle with
        basil
        garlic salt.
3   Bake at 350° 15 to 20 minutes until lightly browned. Set
    aside.
4   Have on hand
        3 c. spaghetti sauce* with sausage
        1½ to 2 c. chopped spinach drained and squeezed dry.

White Sauce

5   Melt
        ¼ c. butter.
6   Add and stir well
        ¼ c. flour.
7   Add and blend until smooth
        1½ c. light cream or milk
        ¼ t. oregano
        dash garlic salt
        ¼ to ½ t. salt
        1 egg yolk.
8   Cook, stirring frequently until thick.

9   Divide half of spaghetti sauce among 4 individual casserole
    dishes (or a flat baking pan)
10 Arrange ½ of eggplant slices over sauce and divide all of the
    spinach among the dishes.

11   Place over spinach

   4 slices Mozzarella cheese (about 4 oz. or 1 slice each
   casserole)

12   Divide remaining sauce and spread over cheese.

13   Arrange remaining eggplant on sauce.

14   Cover with white sauce and sprinkle with oregano.

15   Bake at 350° 12 to 15 minutes to heat through and lightly
  brown sauce.

*See Spaghetti Sauce recipe (page 95)
Serves 4

Ham and Green Bean en Croûte

1   Cut French bread in oblong slices 1″ thick to fit individual
    casserole dishes.
2   Spread with melted butter.
3   Sprinkle lightly with
        basil
        garlic salt
        Parmesan cheese.
4   Bake at 350° for 15 minutes or until crisp and golden.
5   When cool, spread with Boursin cheese.*
6   Place croutons in dishes and divide evenly over
        1½ c. diced (½″ thick) ham
        1 c. cooked green beans.
7   In a mixing bowl beat to blend
        3 eggs
        2 egg yolks
        2 c. heavy cream
        ¼ c. sherry
        ½ t. basil.
8   Divide custard evenly over ham and beans.
9   Divide evenly over all
        1 c. grated Swiss cheese.
10 Bake immediately at 350° until puffed and lightly brown.

*See Boursin Cheese (page 11)
Serves 6

Mexican and Italian Dishes

Peter's Red Hot Chili

1   Brown in 3 T. oil
        2 lb. stew beef.
2   Add
        5 c. water
        1 diced green pepper
        1 diced onion
        1 diced tomato
        1½ T. salt
        2 t. cayenne pepper
        1 T. granulated garlic
        ¼ c. chili powder
        2 T. cumin.
3   Simmer for 2 hours.
4   In a small bowl mix
        1½ c. water
        ⅓ c. cornmeal
        1 6-oz. can tomato paste.
5   Stir cornmeal mixture into chili to thicken.
6   Simmer another 20 minutes.
7   Garnish with sliced raw onions and grated Monterey Jack cheese.

Serves 4

Chicken Burrittos

1   Mix together in a large bowl
        6 c. diced, cooked chicken or turkey
        ½ c. sliced scallions with green tops (or sweet onions)
        ½ to 1 t. chili powder.

2   In another bowl combine
        4 c. sour cream
        ¼ c. minced green olives
        ¼ t. garlic powder.

3   Also have on hand to assemble burittos
        8 to 10 c. grated Monterey Jack or mild Cheddar cheese
        12 large flour tortillas, thaw if frozen
        6 c. taco sauce*
        ½ c. chopped green chilies (or green peppers).

To Assemble

4   Spread ¼ c. of sour cream mixture down the middle of each tortilla.

5   Cover with
        ½ c. of chicken or turkey mixture.

6   Cover chicken with
        ½ c. of cheese
        1 t. of chilies.

7   Dribble over all
        about 2 T. taco sauce.

8   Roll up buritto and place in 9 x 12 baking pan, seam side down, with 2 c. taco sauce in bottom of pan. (You will need 2 pans for 12 burittos.)

9   Cover burittos in pans with remaining cheese and dribble remaining taco sauce over. Sprinkle with chili powder and remaining chilies.

10   Bake at 350° 15 to 20 minutes to melt cheese and heat through.
11   Serve hot with chopped tomatoes and 1 T. each of remaining sour cream and olive mixture and guacamole.**

*See Taco Sauce recipe (page 92)
**See Guacamole recipe (page 91)
Serves 8 to 12.

Chili

1   Brown in a heavy pan
          1 lb. hamburg.
2   Reduce heat to simmer and add
          ½ diced green pepper
          1 diced medium onion
          1 lb. can cooked kidney beans
          1 lb. can stewed tomatoes.
3   Season with
          1 t. crushed red pepper
          2 t. garlic powder
          1½ t. salt
          4 t. chili powder
          2 t. ground cumin
          1 t. oregano
          ¼ t. cinnamon
          dash of cloves.
4   Continue to simmer for ½ hour or until chili is thick.
5   Serve with grated Monterey Jack cheese.

Serves 4

Border Dispute Enchiladas

Prepare in individual casserole dishes. If these are unavailable, layer in a baking pan.

For each individual casserole

1   Overlap in bottom of casserole dish, leaving ½ of each tortilla overhanging each side

   2 fresh or frozen tortillas. (Soak in hot water for a few minutes, if stiff.)

2   In a bowl mix

   ⅓ c. sour cream

   2 T. chopped green olives

   ¼ t. chili powder

   ¼ t. cumin.

3   Spoon the sour cream mixture on to the tortillas.

4   Spread over this

   2 cooked and sliced hot Italian sausages.

5   Fold overhanging tortillas towards the center, overlapping to hold in filling. Secure with 2 long toothpicks.

6   Cover the tortillas with

   ½ c. hot taco sauce*

   ½ c. grated Monterey Jack cheese.

7   Bake until cheese is golden brown.

*See Taco Sauce recipe (page 92)

Guacamole

1   Puree in a food processor until smooth
           3 avocados, peeled and pitted
           1 medium onion
           2 T. lemon juice
           ½ c. hot taco sauce*
           1½ t. cumin powder
           1½ t. chili powder
           1 t. salt
           1 t. garlic salt.
           ½ c. sour cream (optional)
2   Serve with tacos or chips or spread on tostadas.

*See Taco Sauce recipe (page 92)
Makes about 2 cups

Chivichangas

1   Spread on each flour tortilla
           3 T. chili
           1 T. diced raw onion
           1 T. diced tomato
           2 t. diced green olives
           2 T. grated Monterey Jack cheese.
2   Roll the tortilla firmly.
3   Fry in 2 inches of hot oil (just short of smoking) until brown and crisp.
4   Garnish with shredded lettuce, chopped fresh tomatoes, and taco sauce.*

*See Taco Sauce recipe (page 92)

Taco Sauce

Not So Hot

1   In a heavy kettle, simmer for ½ hour

        1 lb. can stewed tomatoes

        1 8-oz. can tomato sauce

        1 chopped onion

        1 chopped green pepper

        2 t. granulated garlic

        1 t. cumin powder

        1 t. chili powder

        1½ t. salt

        1 T. lemon juice

        ½ t. cayenne pepper.

2   Puree in blender or food processor until sauce is just slightly chunky.

Hot Sauce

Add an extra teaspoon (or more!) cayenne pepper to step 2.

Tostadas

1   Lay desired number of corn tortillas on a cookie sheet.

2   Layer on each tortilla in order

        ½ c. refried beans

        2 T. diced raw onion

        2 T. diced tomatoes

        1 T. diced olives

        ⅓ c. hot taco sauce*

        ½ c. grated Monterey Jack cheese.

3   Bake in a hot oven (400°) until cheese is browned.

4   Serve with guacamole or sour cream.

*See Taco Sauce recipe above.

Red Eye Chili Pie

1   Divide evenly among 4 individual casserole dishes
        4 to 6 cups chili.*
2   Divide evenly over chili
        1 c. chopped onion
        ½ c. chopped green olives
        2 chopped tomatoes.
3   In a measuring cup combine and let stand 5 minutes to sour
        1½ t. vinegar
        light cream or milk to make ½ c.
4   In a bowl combine
        ½ c. cornmeal
        ⅓ c. flour
        ¼ c. whole wheat flour
        ½ t. baking powder
        ¼ t. baking soda
        ¼ t. salt
        ½ t. chili powder.
5   Add sour cream to cornmeal mixture with
        1 egg
        2 T. oil.
6   Blend well, then stir in
        1 c. grated Cheddar cheese.
7   Divide corn bread evenly over casseroles.
8   Bake at 375° 12 to 15 minutes until corn bread is golden and
        chili is hot.

*See Chili recipe page 89)
Serves 4

Casserole Enchiladas

1   In a 9"x9" baking dish, spread
        ½ c. hot taco sauce*

2   Cover with
        4 fresh or frozen corn tortillas.

3   In a small bowl mix
        1½ c. cottage cheese
        2 t. chili powder
        2 t. cumin powder
        1 diced onion.

4   Spread cottage cheese mixture on tortillas.

5   Add
        2 c. grated Monterey Jack cheese.

6   Cover with
        1 c. hot taco sauce.

7   Layer on top
        4 more corn tortillas.

8   Spread with
        ½ c. taco sauce.

9   Sprinkle on top
        ½ c. grated Monterey Jack cheese.

10   Bake at 350° until bubbly and cheese starts to brown.

*See Taco Sauce recipe (page 92)
Serves 6

Spaghetti Sauce

1   Heat in a heavy soup kettle
         2 T. olive oil.
2   Add and sauté over medium high heat until tender (10 to 15 minutes)
         1 c. chopped green pepper
         1½ c. chopped onion
         2 minced garlic cloves (or use 1 t. garlic powder).
3   Add and combine well
         6 c. crushed or stewed tomatoes
         ¼ c. red wine
         2 t. basil
         2 t. oregano
         1 t. sugar or honey
         ½ to 1 t. chili powder
         ⅛ t. cayenne pepper
         1 t. salt or to taste
         1 c. tomato puree or sauce.
4   Simmer, stirring occasionally, over low heat for 2 hours.
5   Season to taste.
6   Use as a base for Italian dishes or add cooked sausage or meatballs or hamburger and serve on spaghetti.

Makes about 8 cups.

Cheese and Spinach Manicotti

1   Have on hand

        8 c. spaghetti sauce*

2   Combine well

        2 lb. cottage cheese or ricotta (drain if soupy)

        ¼ lb. grated Mozzarella cheese

        ½ c. Parmesan cheese

        2 eggs

        1 c. chopped, cooked and squeezed dry spinach (1 box frozen)

        ¼ c. dry seasoned bread crumbs

        ½ t. basil

        dash pepper

        dash nutmeg.

3   Stuff into 12 to 16 manicotti noodles (raw, not cooked).

4   Spread about ⅓ of spaghetti sauce in a 9"x12" baking dish.

5   Arrange stuffed manicotti in pan and cover with remaining sauce.

6   Bake covered at 350° for 45 minutes.

7   Uncover and top with

        1 lb. thin sliced Mozzarella cheese.

8   Bake 5 to 10 minutes more to melt cheese.

*See Spaghetti Sauce recipe (page 95)
Serves 4 to 6

Parmesan Crescents

1   Puree in a food processor
      2 c. cottage cheese
      ½ c. cold butter, cut in chunks
      ⅛ t. salt
      ½ t. basil.
2   Transfer to mixing bowl and mix in until well combined
      ½ c. whole wheat flour
      2½ c. flour.
3   Divide dough into 6 balls and flatten each ball into a 4″ circle. Chill 1 hour.
4   Have on hand for rolling out dough
      1 c. melted butter
      2 to 3 c. Parmesan cheese.
5   Sprinkle baking sheets with cheese. Preheat oven to 375°.
6   Roll each circle of dough to a circle 12 to 15″ in diameter, using a lot of cheese to keep it from sticking and tearing.
7   Spread circle with melted butter, lightly, but evenly.
8   Cut circle in 6 or 8 pieces and roll up from wide end into crescent shape. Arrange on sheets close together.
9   Bake at 375° 15 to 20 minutes until browned and crisp looking. (The cheese on the sheets gets very brown and smells slightly burned, but don't worry).

Crescents freeze well.

Makes 36 to 48 crescents.

Chicken Parmesan

1   Have on hand
            2 c. spaghetti sauce.*
2   With a meat mallet, between plastic wrap, pound to an even
      thickness
            6 skinned boned chicken breasts.
3   Sprinkle inside of each breast lightly with
            oregano.
4   Roll each chicken breast around
            ½ c. grated Mozzarella cheese.
5   Divide ½ of sauce among 6 individual casserole dishes or into
      one large enough for all chicken breasts.
6   Place chicken seam side down on sauce. Cover each with sauce
      and
            ¼ c. grated Mozzarella cheese
            1 T. Parmesan cheese.
7   Bake at 350° 15 to 20 minutes or until chicken is just cooked.

*See Spaghetti Sauce recipe (page 95)
Serves 6

Italian Meatball Sub

1   Mix together in a bowl
          2 lb. ground chuck
          2 c. bread crumbs
          1 minced onion
          ⅓ c. Burgundy
          ¼ c. grated Parmesan cheese
          1½ t. basil
          ½ t. thyme
          ½ t. granulated garlic.

2   Roll into balls and place in a baking dish.

3   Bake in 375° oven until just done (about 30 to 40 minutes).

4   Slice a grinder roll in half.

5   Layer bottom of each roll with
          3 meatballs cut in half
          ½ c. spaghetti sauce*
          3 slices of Provolone or Mozarella cheese
          light sprinkle of Parmesan cheese.

6   Broil until cheese is melted.

*See Spaghetti Sauce recipe (page 95)
Serves 4 to 6

Sausage and Spinach Stuffed Shells

1   Have on hand
        2 c. spaghetti sauce*.
2   In a small frying pan heat
        1 T. olive oil.
3   Add and sauté until tender
        ½ c. chopped onion
        1 small minced garlic clove.
4   Combine onion and garlic in a bowl with
        1 lb. ground cooked sweet Italian sausage (about 1¼ lb. raw)
        1 c. cooked and squeezed dry chopped spinach (1 box frozen)
        2 T. Parmesan cheese
        1 egg
        1 T. heavy cream
        ½ t. basil
        ¼ t. oregano.
5   Cook large shells, 12 to 15 (cook a few extra in case some get damaged).

White Sauce

6   Melt in a saucepan
        2 T. butter.
7   Add and stir in
        2 T. flour.
8   Add and stir in
        1 c. milk.
9   Cook and stir until thick.

10   Remove from heat and stir in
          1 T. heavy cream
          ¼ t. oregano
          ¼ t. salt.

11   On the bottom of 4 individual casserole dishes or one large
      enough to hold 12 shells, spread a layer of spaghetti sauce,
      reserving ½ c.
12   Stuff sausage and spinach filling evenly into cooked shells and
      place on sauce in casserole.
13   Spoon white sauce evenly over shells.
14   Spoon a thin line of reserved spaghetti sauce over white sauce.
15   Cover evenly with
          ½ c. Parmesan cheese.
16   Cover loosely with foil (use toothpicks to keep it from touching
      shells). Bake at 350° 25 to 30 minutes.

See Spaghetti Sauce recipe (page 95)
Serves 4

Venetian Lasagna

1   Melt in a heavy soup kettle
      2 T. butter
      1 T. oil.

2   Add and sauté until tender
      1 c. chopped onion
      1 minced garlic clove.

3   Add and stir to combine well
      ½ lb. ground cooked turkey or chicken
      1 c. cooked and drained spinach (1 box frozen)
      ½ c. chicken broth
      ½ t. salt
      ¼ t. nutmeg
      2 c. sliced mushrooms
      dash pepper.

4   Bring to a boil, then turn heat to low and simmer 20 to 30 minutes to absorb all liquid.

5   Transfer to a bowl to cool.

6   Cook lasagna noodles to make 3 layers in a 9x9″ baking dish.

White Sauce

7   Melt in a saucepan
      ½ c. butter.

8   Stir in
      ½ c. flour.

9   Add and stir in until smooth
      2½ c. light cream or milk.

10 Cook and stir until thick.

11   Stir in and remove from heat
          ½ c. heavy cream
          ¼ t. oregano
          ½ t. salt
          dash pepper.

12   Cover bottom of oiled baking dish (9x9″) with cooked lasagna
        noodles.
13   To turkey and spinach mixture, add and blend well
          2 T. heavy cream
          1 egg
          2 T. Parmesan cheese.
14   Spread ½ of turkey and spinach mixture on noodles. Cover
        with
          ⅓ of sauce
          ⅓ c. Parmesan cheese.
15   Repeat layers once more. Cover last layer with more noodles.
16   Spread remaining sauce on top of noodles and spinach with
              1 c. grated Mozarella cheese
              ⅓ c. Parmesan cheese.
17   Bake at 350° for 30 to 40 minutes until top is browned and
        filling bubbles at edges.

Serves 4 to 6

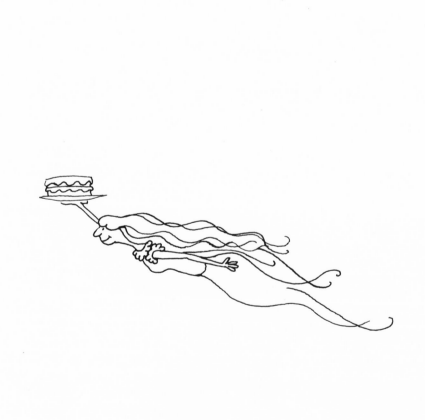

Desserts

Desserts are my passion; when people ask me how I come up with so many different ideas, all I can answer is that I make what I want to taste, and I seem just to know how to arrive at that taste. Of course, it's a step-by-step process, and experience has taught me a lot and led me on to new combinations. Sometimes I really get carried away (as in Candy Bar Pie), but the end result always seems worth it. I'm satisfied and those who eat these desserts seem to be also. Making up a recipe is easy for me. It's writing it all down that is hard. I've tried not to assume too much when it comes to the "how to put it together," but certain basics—like what it means to cream butter until fluffy or beat egg whites until stiff—I think you know already. This shouldn't be your only cookbook. A good all-purpose book like *Joy of Cooking* or *Fannie Farmer* (my favorites) should be in everyone's collection for reference and definition of terms.

I shall mention a few rules I have gone by in these recipes. Rule 1: I don't sift. I mix the dry ingredients in a bowl with a wire whisk to fluff and evenly distribute and combine them. If you do like to sift, measure first, not after, for these recipes.

Rule 2: I always add some gelatin to cream pies to make sure they will set up in time to serve. I don't have time to let a pie chill overnight so that it will be stiff enough to cut. Also, I've found that if your cooked custard mixture curdles, you can whip it in a blender until smooth, and though it would be thin without the gelation, with it it will still set up and be creamy.

Rule 3: I always use springform pans becuase they are easy, but if you don't have them, cut a piece of wax paper the shape of the bottom of your pan, grease the pan and the paper, and the cake will always come out. Nothing aggravates me more than a cake breaking up as I try to get it to come out of the pan.

Rule 4: I consider almonds, pecans, and walnuts virtually interchangeable. What you like best is one thing, but what you have on hand can make just as perfectly a delicious dessert. (Peanuts don't qualify here, as they can be dreadful in some recipes.) I am sorry to see people dashing to the store for pecans when they have almonds, or for dark corn syrup when they have honey, or for apricot jam when they have orange marmalade. Of course, it will make the recipe a bit different, but you learn a lot that way.

Rule 5: just use common sense. I use butter or margarine; oil won't work well. Honey is sweeter than corn syrup, and so use a little less. If you have light corn syrup and want dark, add some molasses.

Experiment, but do it gradually and learn what you can get away with without taking any real big chances. If something flops, you can always make it into something else. Many times a fallen cake has become bread pudding, or a parfait, layered with fruit and pudding or a trifle. I've always learned from it and had fun, and isn't that what it's all about?   J.P.

Graham Cracker Crust

1   Combine well
            1⅓ c. graham cracker crumbs
            ¼ c. brown sugar
            ¼ c. melted butter

(Optional ingredients

    1 t. grated lemon or orange peel

    1 t. vanilla

    1 T. instant coffee

    2 to 4 T. ground peanuts, almonds or walnuts

    2 T. cocoa powder

    ½ t. cinnamon or nutmeg.)

2   Pat in 9 or 10" pie pan and bake at 375° 12 to 15 minutes until lightly browned.

3   Cool before filling.

Pie Crust

1   With a pastry blender or fork, combine until mixture looks like oatmeal;

    1¼ c. white flour

    ¼ c. whole wheat flour

    ½ t. salt

    1 to 4 T. sugar

    ⅓ c. cold butter or margarine.

2   Mix well

    1 egg

    ⅓ c. cold milk or water.

3   Add liquid to dry ingredients, 1 T. at a time just until mixture forms a ball (may not need all of it).

4   Form in a ball, flatten and roll out on floured board.

5   Makes enough for 1 10" pie or quiche pan or a double crust 9" pie.

Peach Date Crunch Pie

1   Combine in a saucepan and cook over low heat 20 minutes or
    until thick and soft
   ½ lb. dates, chopped
   1½ c. raisins
   ¾ brown sugar
   ¼ c. maple syrup or honey
   1 T. lemon rind, grated
   ⅔ c. apple juice.

2   Cool to room temperature, then stir in
   2 c. fresh or canned peaches, sliced.

3   In a mixing bowl combine until well mixed
   ¾ c. white flour
   ¾ c. whole wheat flour
   1½ c. oatmeal
   1 c. brown sugar
   1 c. chopped almonds
   1 c. soft butter
   ½ t. salt
   ½ t. baking soda
   1 T. lemon rind, grated
   1 t. vanilla
   1 t. nutmeg.

4   Pat one half of oatmeal mixture into greased 10″ springform
    pan.

5   Spread date mix and cover with remaining oatmeal mixture.

6   Bake at 350° 45 to 50 minutes.

7   Cool. Serve with whipped cream and a sprinkle of nutmeg.

Serves 12

Banana or Coconut Cream Pie

1   Combine in top of double boiler
        4 beaten eggs
        2 c. light cream or milk
        ½ c. plus 1 T. sugar
        1½ t. plain gelatin.
2   Cook over boiling water, stirring often until custard is thick
     and coats a metal spoon.
3   Pour into blender and blend until smooth with
        1 large banana
        1½ t. vanilla.
4   Pour into large bowl, cover with plastic, and chill. Stir occa-
     sionally to avoid lumps.
5   In a small bowl, whip until stiff
        1 c. heavy cream.
6   Divide the whipped cream in half:
        Fold ½ of the whipped cream into cooled custard.
        To remaining cream, add and mix in 2 T. powdered
        sugar for garnish.
7   Pour custard (whisk if necessary until smooth) into baked and
     cooled graham cracker or regular pie crust. Mound custard in
     the middle.
8   Garnish with reserved sweetened whipped cream and banana
     chips. Chill until stiff before serving.

For Coconut Cream Pie use ½ c. sweetened coconut instead of banana
and ½ t. almond or coconut extract and ½ t. vanilla in custard. Use
the same flavorings in the whipped cream and garnish with toasted
coconut.

Serves 8

Mandarin Chocolate Chip Pie

1   Combine in medium bowl and beat until well mixed
        5 eggs
        ¾ c. orange marmalade
        ½ c. sugar
        1 T. Cointreau or Triple Sec or 1 t. orange extract
        ¼ c. melted butter
        dash salt.

2   Fold in gently
        ¾ c. chocolate chips
        1 c. mandarin oranges, drained.

3   Pour into unbaked 9″ pie shell.

4   Bake at 400° for 10 minutes, then turn oven to 350° for 35 to 45 minutes until set.

Serves 8 to 10

Almond Cookie Tart

Crust

1   Mix with mixer or spoon until well blended
        ½ c. soft butter
        ½ c. brown sugar
        1 beaten egg
        ¾ c. white flour
        ¼ c. whole wheat flour
        ½ t. baking powder
        ½ t. almond extract
        ½ t. vanilla
        ½ c. finely chopped toasted almonds.

2   Press evenly into greased 10" springform pan with floured fingers.

3   Bake at 350° for 20 minutes or until set and beginning to brown.

Filling

4   Combine with mixer or whisk while crust cooks

> 3 eggs
> 1½ c. brown sugar
> ¼ c. flour
> ¾ t. baking powder
> ½ t. salt
> ½ t. vanilla
> 2 T. Amaretto or 1 t. almond extract
> 2 c. chopped toasted almonds.

5   Pour filling over hot crust and bake 35 to 45 minutes until set and knife inserted near middle comes out clean.

6   Cool to room temperature, remove from pan and chill.

Topping

7   Whip until stiff

> 1¼ c. heavy cream
> ¼ c. powdered sugar
> 2 T. Amaretto or 1 t. almond extract.

8   Spread on before cutting or serve over individual pieces. Sprinkle with toasted almonds.

Serves 10 to 12.

Mocha Chiffon Pie

1   Melt in a small pan over low heat
        3 squares unsweetened chocolate.
2   Cool to room temperature.
3   In another small pan combine
        ½ c. cold coffee
        1 T. gelatin.
4   Let stand for 5 minutes, then heat to dissolve gelatin.
5   In a mixing bowl, beat at high speed until thick and lemon colored
        ½ c. egg yolks (6)
        ½ c. sugar.
6   Add gradually at low speed
        coffee and gelatin mixture
        cooled chocolate
        ¼ c. Coffee Brandy or Kahlua.
7   Cool to room temperature.
8   In another bowl, whip (with clean beaters) until stiff
        4 egg whites.
9   Fold egg whites carefully into mocha mixture.
10 In the same bowl, beat until stiff (no need to wash beaters)
        1 c. heavy cream.
11 Reserve ½ c. of the whipped cream for garnish. Fold the remainder into the mocha mixture. Chill until it begins to set if it is soupy.
12 Pour into baked and cooled chocolate graham cracker crust.* Mound the mocha mixture in the middle to accommodate all the filling. Refrigerate.
13 To the reserved whipped cream, add and whisk until thick
        2 T. powdered sugar
        2 T. Coffee Brandy or Kahlua.

14   Pipe whipped cream on the pie with a pastry bag or drop dollops with a teaspoon. Decorate with chocolate curls or chocolate chips.

15   Chill 2 hours or until completely set.

This pie can be frozen. Let stand 30 minutes at room temperature before cutting.

See Graham Cracker Crust recipe (page 106)
Serves 8

Lemon Mint Pie

1   Bake and chill an 8 or 9″ graham cracker crust with lemon rind added.

2   In a small saucepan combine
        ⅓ c. fresh lemon juice
        1 t. plain gelatin.

3   Let stand 5 minutes, then heat to dissolve gelatin.

4   In a medium bowl combine
        1 can sweetened condensed milk
        4 egg yolks
        lemon and gelatin mix.

5   Pour in pie crust.

6   Over top of pie filling, pour and swirl into the top ½″
        1 to 2 T. green Creme de Menthe.

7   Whip together until stiff and spread over pie
        1¼ c. heavy cream
        ¼ c. powdered sugar
        2 T. green Creme de Menthe.

8   Chill for 2 hours and garnish with fresh mint.

Serves 8

Brownie Chip Pie

1   Add to mixing bowl in order given and blend well

        3 eggs

        1¼ c. sugar

        1 T. Creme de Menthe or Kahlua or Amaretto

        1 c. flour

        ½ c. cocoa powder

        ¼ t. salt

        ¾ t. baking powder

        ½ c. melted and cooled butter

        ½ c. small chocolate chips.

2   Spread in greased 9″ springform pan.

3   Bake at 350° 25 to 30 minutes.

4   Cool 15 minutes. Remove from pan and cool to room temperature.

5   For topping, whip until very stiff (don't overbeat or it will curdle)

        1¼ c. heavy cream

        ¼ c. powdered sugar

        2 to 4 T. Creme de Menthe or Kahlua or Amaretto.

6   Spread topping over pie and sprinkle with more chocolate chips.

Serves 8 to 10

Brownie Pie Variations

Rum Fudge
1   Use rum in brownie mixture and in whipped cream.
2   Add 2 T. cocoa powder to whipped cream.

Mocha Fudge
1   Use Coffee Brandy in brownie mixture and in whipped cream.
2   Add 2 T. cocoa powder and 1 T. instant coffee to whipped cream.

Peanut Fudge
1   Use Creme de Cocoa in brownie mixture and in whipped cream.
2   Spread brownie mixture with ¼ to ½ c. creamy peanut butter.
3   Cover with whipped cream (add 2 T. cocoa powder, if desired) and sprinkle with chocolate chips and peanuts.

Coconut Fudge
1   Use Creme de Cocoa and 1 T. coconut extract in brownie mixture.
2   Add 2 T. cocoa powder and 1 T. coconut extract to whipped cream.
3   Sprinkle top with toasted coconut.

Brandy Alexander
1   Use brandy in brownie mixture and add ¼ t. nutmeg.
2   Add 2 T. brandy and 2 T. Creme de Cocoa to whipped cream.
3   Sprinkle top of whipped cream with nutmeg and chocolate chips.

Happy Fruit Pie

1   Bake and cool a 9″ pie crust*.

2   Have on hand

       2 c. unsweetened pineapple juice.

3   Pour 1½ c. juice into a bowl and refrigerate. To remaining ½ c. add in a small saucepan

       4 t. gelatin

       ¼ c. sugar.

4   Let stand 5 minutes to soften gelatin, then heat to dissolve gelatin and sugar.

5   Add gelatin mixture to chilled pineapple juice with

       2 T. Triple Sec or 1 t. orange extract.

6   Chill until mixture begins to set, but is not stiff.

7   In another bowl, whip until stiff

       1 c. heavy cream.

8   Fold half of whipped cream (about 1 c.) into gelatin. To remaining half add and whisk until thick

       2 T. powdered sugar

       1 T. Triple Sec.

9   Reserve sweetened whipped cream for garnish.

10   Fold into gelatin

       2 c. sliced fresh strawberries (or 1 c. strawberries and 1 c. sliced peaches)

       1 c. fresh blueberries

       ½ c. crushed pineapple, drained.

11   Pour into cooled pie crust and garnish with reserved whipped cream and some fresh strawberries. Chill well.

See Pie Crust recipe (page 107)

Serves 8 to 10

Eggnog Mousse Pie

1   Bake and cool a 9" graham cracker crust.*

2   Combine in a small pan and let stand for 5 minutes
        ½ c. cold water
        1 T. plain gelatin.

3   Heat to dissolve gelatin.

4   In a mixing bowl beat together on high speed until very thick and pale yellow
        6 egg yolks
        1 c. sugar.

5   Blend in gradually
        ½ c. dark rum (brandy or bourbon is also good).

6   On low speed, blend in gelatin mixture, making sure it is evenly mixed.

7   In another bowl, whip until stiff
        2 c. heavy cream.

8   Reserve 1 c. of whipped cream for garnish. Fold remainder into egg mixture and pour into cool pie crust. (Chill until partially set, if it is soupy.)

9   To reserved whipped cream, add and mix in well
        2 T. powdered sugar
        2 T. rum.

10 Decorate pie with reserved whipped cream and sprinkle whole pie lightly with nutmeg. Chill until stiff and cut with a hot knife.

*See Graham Cracker Crust recipe (page 106)
Serves 8 to 10

German Chocolate Pie

Crust

1   Mix well, pat in 9″ pie pan and bake at 375° 12 to 15 minutes

        1¼ c. graham cracker crumbs

        2 T. cocoa

        ¼ c. coconut

        ¼ c. brown sugar

        ⅓ c. melted butter

        ½ t. coconut extract.

Topping

2   Mix well, toast at 350° for 10 minutes, cool and set aside,

        ½ c. coconut

        2 T. chopped pecans

        1 T. melted butter.

Filling

3   Beat at high speed until thick and light yellow

        6 egg yolks

        ½ c. sugar

        1 t. coconut extract.

4   Melt over hot water, then cool to room temperature

        2 squares unsweetened chocolate.

5   Meanwhile combine in small saucepan

        ⅓ c. water

        1 T. gelatin.

6   Let stand 5 minutes, then heat to dissolve gelatin.

7   Blend gelatin and chocolate into egg mixture and combine well.

8   Whip until stiff and fold in

        4 egg whites.

9   Beat until stiff and fold in

        1 c. heavy cream.

10   Pour filling into cooled crust and sprinkle with cooled topping. (Chill filling until partially set, if it is soupy, before pouring into cooled crust.) Chill until stiff before cutting.

Serves 8

Kahlua or Peach Brandy Pecan Pie

1   Cream in a medium bowl
      ¼ c. soft butter
      ⅔ c. sugar.
2   Add one at a time and blend in
      5 large eggs.
3   Add and blend well
      dash of salt
      1¼ c. dark corn syrup
      ½ c. Kahlua
      ½ c. chopped pecans
      ½ t. vanilla
      1 T. instant coffee.
4   Pour in unbaked pie crust and bake at 350° for 45 to 50 minutes. Cool.
5   For topping, whip until stiff
      1 c. heavy cream
      2 T. powdered sugar
      2 T. Kahlua.
6   Top each serving of pie with whipped cream and sprinkle with a few nuts.
7   For Peach Brandy pie, use Peach Brandy instead of Kahlua and omit the instant coffee. Also, 1 c. chopped peaches (fresh or canned) can be added.

Serves 6 to 8

Candy Bar Pie

Crust

1   Mix well with a fork and press into 9″ pie pan

       1 c. crushed chocolate cookies (½ box)

       3 T. brown sugar

       3 T. finely chopped peanuts or pecans

       ¼ c. melted butter

       ½ t. vanilla.

2   Bake at 350° for 15 minutes. Chill well.

Topping

3   Combine in a saucepan and cook over low heat until thick, stirring constantly,

       2 T. butter

       ½ c. brown sugar

       ½ c. light cream

       1 egg yolk

       1 T. cornstarch.

4   Divide in half. To one half add

       ½ square unsweetened chocolate, melted

       ½ t. vanilla

       1 T. brandy.

5   To other half add

       ½ t. vanilla

       1 T. Creme de Cocoa.

6   Let both cool to room temperature.

Filling

7   Combine in top of double boiler

       1 T. gelatin softened in ¼ c. water

       1 c. light cream

       3 eggs yolks

       ½ c. brown sugar

       2 T. cocoa powder.

8 Cook over boiling water, stirring frequently until custard is thick and coats a metal spoon. Remove from heat and stir in

   1 T. brandy

   1 t. vanilla.

9 Cool, stirring frequently, but don't let it gel. When cool fold in

   1 c. heavy cream, whipped until stiff.

10 Spread the topping with Creme de Cocoa into the bottom of chilled crust and sprinkle with

   2 T. chopped peanuts or pecans.

11 Pour filling over nuts. Chill well until set.

12 Spread remaining chocolate topping over filling and sprinkle with

   2 T. chopped peanuts or pecans.

13 Chill very well and cut with a hot knife.

Serve 8 to 10

Peanut Butter and Jelly Pie

Crust

1   Mix well, pat into a 9" pie plate and bake at 375° 12 to 15 minutes

    1¼ c. graham cracker crumbs

    ¼ c. brown sugar

    ¼ c. finely chopped peanuts

    ⅓ c. melted butter.

Filling

2   Combine and let stand 5 minutes to soften gelatin

    ½ c. strong grape juice*

    1 T. gelatin.

3   Heat in small saucepan to dissolve gelatin and add to

    1½ c. strong grape juice*

4   Chill until partially set, but not firm.

5   Spread bottom of cooled crust with

    ½ c. peanut butter (heat in a double boiler if it is too thick to spread).

6   Pour gelatin over peanut butter and chill until firm.

Topping

7   Whip until stiff

    1¼ c. heavy cream

    ¼ c. powdered sugar

    1 t. vanilla.

8   Fold in

    ½ c. chopped peanuts.

9   Spread topping over gelatin and sprinkle with

    2 T. peanuts, whole or chopped.

10   Chill well.

*For strong grape juice, use frozen concentrate and add only ⅔ the amount of water called for.

Serves 8 to 10

Mocha Macaroon Pie

1   Whip at high speed until it forms soft peaks
           5 egg whites.
2   Add and whip to stiff peaks
           1 c. minus 2 T. sugar
           1 t. vanilla
           2 t. instant coffee
           ½ t. almond extract.
3   Add, folding gently by hand,
           6 oz. grated unsweetened chocolate
           1 c. graham cracker crumbs
           ¼ c. coconut
           1 t. baking powder.
4   Pour into greased and floured 9" springform pan and bake at
     350° 30 to 35 minutes.
5   Cool 15 minutes, then chill.
6   For topping, whip until stiff
           1½ c. heavy cream
           ¼ c. confectioners sugar
           1 T. instant coffee
           1 t. vanilla
           ½ t. almond extract.
7   Spread topping over chilled pie. Sprinkle with
           2 T. grated chocolate
           2 T. toasted coconut.

Serves 8 to 10

Peanut Butter Cup Pie

Crust

1   Bake and cool a 9″ graham cracker crust* including

         2 T. cocoa powder

         2 T. ground peanuts

         1 t. vanilla.

Mousse

2   Heat over low heat in a small saucepan (to dissolve sugar)

         ½ c. sugar

         ⅓ c. Creme de Cocoa.

3   Add

         5 squares unsweetened chocolate.

4   Stir to melt.

5   Transfer to a bowl and stir in

         ¼ c. heavy cream.

6   Let mixture cool to room temperature.

7   Beat until stiff

         2 c. heavy cream.

8   Reserve 1 cup, then fold remainder into cooled chocolate mixture.

9   In another bowl, beat until stiff but not dry

         3 egg whites.

10   Fold into cooled chocolate mixture.

11   Fold in carefully

         ½ c. chopped peanuts.

12   Melt in the top of a double boiler, then spread in cooled crust,

         ⅓ c. creamy peanut butter.

13   Pour chocolate mousse over cooled peanut butter in crust.

14   Sprinkle with
       ¼ c. chopped peanuts.
15   To reserved whipped cream add and whisk until stiff
       2 T. powdered sugar
       1 t. vanilla.
16   Decorate pie with whipped cream.

See Graham Cracker Crust recipe (page 106)
Serves 8 to 10

Chocolate Pecan Cream Pie

Crust

1   Mix well and pat in 9″ pie pan and bake at 375° 12 to 15
minutes and chill well

        1¼ c. graham cracker crumbs

        ¼ c. brown sugar

        2 T. cocoa

        2 T. chopped pecans

        ⅓ c. butter

        ½ t. vanilla.

Filling

2   Mix in top of double boiler:

        1 c. light cream

        ½ c. brown sugar

        ⅓ c. dark corn syrup

        1 egg

        1 egg yolk.

3   Cook over boiling water until thickened, stirring frequently.

4   Combine

        ¼ c. milk

        1 T. gelatin.

5   Let stand 5 minutes and stir into cream mixture to dissolve
gelatin.

6   Stir in until melted

        2 squares unsweetened chocolate

        1 T. butter

        1 t. vanilla.

7   Transfer to bowl and chill until it begins to mound, but is not
stiff. Stir a few times to avoid lumps.

8   Whip until stiff
          1½ c. heavy cream.

9   Reserve 1 c. and fold remainder into filling with
          ½ c. chopped pecans.

10   Pour filling in cooled pie crust.

11   To reserved whipped cream, add and combine by whisking
          1 T. powdered sugar
          1 t. vanilla.

12   Garnish pie with
          whipped cream
          ¼ c. pecan pieces.

13   Chill well before cutting.

Serves 8

Pumpkin Cheesecake

1   Prepare graham cracker pie crust*, adding ½ t. cinnamon. Pat into 10" springform pan, but do not bake.

2   Cream well in a large bowl on high speed
       1½ lb. cream cheese
       ½ c. brown sugar
       ¼ c. maple syrup or light molasses
       1½ t. vanilla.

3   Add and blend well, scraping the bowl often and incorporating all lumps;
       1 c. canned pumpkin
       2 T. flour
       ½ t. cinnamon
       ½ t. nutmeg
       ¼ t. cloves
       ⅛ t. allspice
       ⅛ t. ginger.

4   Add one at a time, blending well after each addition,
       4 eggs.

5   Add and beat well until fluffy
       ¼ c. melted and cooled butter.

6   Bake at 325° for 30 minutes. Turn off oven and leave cheesecake in oven for 30 minutes more. Cool to room temperature. Chill well before cutting.

7   Serve with whipped cream and sprinkle of cinnamon.

*See Graham Cracker Pie Crust recipe (page 106)
Serves 12

Cheesecake

Crust

1   Mix with a fork

   1 c. graham cracker crumbs

   ¼ c. brown sugar

   ¼ c. melted butter

   ¼ t. cinnamon.

2   Reserve 2 T. mixture for the topping and pat the rest into the bottom of 10" springform pan.

Cheesecake

3   Cream well at high speed

   ½ c. soft butter.

4   Add and beat on high until fluffy

   2 lb. cream cheese.

5   Add gradually continuing to beat (and scrape sides of bowl occasionally) at high speed;

   1 c. plus 2 T. sugar.

6   Add one at a time

   4 eggs.

7   Blend in and whip until fluffy

   ½ t. vanilla

   1 T. lemon juice.

8   Pour into crust, smooth top and sprinkle with reserved crumbs.

9   Bake at 300° for 35 minutes. Turn off oven and leave in oven 35 minutes. Cool to room temperature, then chill 2 to 4 hours before cutting.

Serves 12

Cheesecake Variations

Maple Pecan Cheesecake

1   Add ¼ c. ground pecans to crust and double vanilla in cheesecake.
2   Spread cheesecake in pan and drizzle ¼ c. dark maple syrup over the top and marble into ½" of batter with a knife.
3   Sprinkle ⅓ c. chopped pecans over top of cake and bake as usual.

Mocha Chip Cheesecake

1   Add 2 T. instant coffee to crust.
2   While mixing cheesecake mixture, combine and let stand in a measuring cup
        2 T. instant coffee
        2 T. coffee brandy
        1 t. vanilla.
3   When cheesecake is mixed, add coffee and brandy mixture and blend in well.
4   Also stir in 1 c. chocolate chips. Spread cheesecake in pan, sprinkle with more chips and bake as usual.

Coconut Chocolate Chip Cheesecake

1   Add ¼ c. coconut to crust.
2   Add 1 T. coconut extract to cheesecake mixture and stir in ½ c. chocolate chips and ½ c. chopped coconut.
3   Sprinkle top with more coconut and bake as usual.

German Chocolate Cheesecake

1   Add ¼ c. coconut and 2 T. cocoa powder to crust.
2   To cheesecake, add 1 T. coconut extract and 1½ squares unsweetened chocolate, melted and cooled.
3   Sprinkle top liberally with coconut and bake as usual.

Cappuccino Cheesecake

1   Add extra ¼ t. cinnamon and 2 T. instant coffee to crust.
2   Stir into cheesecake mixture:
       2 T. instant coffee
       2 T. Coffee Brandy
       ½ t. cinnamon
       ½ c. grated unsweetened chocolate.
3   Sprinkle top with cinnamon and bake as usual.

Chocolate Cheesecake

1   Add 2 T. cocoa to crust (plus 2 T. ground almonds for Chocoalte Almond.)
2   Add 4 squares unsweetened chocolate to cheesecake, melted and cooled (plus 1 t. almond extract or 1 T. Amaretto for Chocolate Almond.)
3   Sprinkle with crumbs (or almonds) and bake as usual.

Blueberry Cheesecake

1   To finished cheesecake, add and blend well
       1 T. fresh grated lemon rind.
2   Fold in carefully
       2 c. fresh dry blueberries.
3   Bake as usual.

Strawberry Mousse Cake

1   Sift 3 times and set aside
       2½ c. flour
       ¼ c. whole wheat flour (or use all white flour)
       3 t. baking powder
       ½ t. salt.

2   In a mixing bowl, beat until thick and lemon colored
       12 egg yolks
       2 c. sugar.

3   Add gradually, scraping the bowl often and blending in well;
       1 c. hot light cream or milk
       1 t. vanilla.

4   Fold in the sifted flour mixture (in 3 batches) gently and just until all white patches are incorporated.

5   Pour into *ungreased* 10″ Bundt type pan or angel food cake pan. Bake at 350° 55 to 60 minutes.

6   Invert pan over a wine bottle to cool completely.

7   While cake bakes and cools, prepare ½ recipe fresh strawberry mousse* and chill until partially set but not stiff.

8   When cake is cooled cut a 1″ slice off the top and remove. Then slice 1″ slice from the bottom and remove.

9   Spread the bottom slice with
       2 to 4 T. apricot jam.

10   Replace middle layer onto bottom slice.

11   Around the hole in the center, left by the cake pan, slice a circle ½″ from the hole. Slice another circle ½″ from the outside of the cake. Remove the cake between the slices but leave ½″ of cake at the bottom. This moat is for the chilled mousse.

12   Pour chilled mousse into this moat.

13   Spread top slice with 2 to 4 T. apricot jam and replace on top of cake, covering the mousse-filled moat.

14   Chill cake 1 to 2 hours to completely jell the mousse.

15   Melt in a double boiler
       1 c. apricot jam.

16   Brush melted jam over the cake to cover completely.

17   Decorate with reserve whipped cream (from mousse) and fresh strawberries.

Is also very good with peaches or raspberries.

See Fresh Strawberry Mousse recipe (page 156)
Serves 12 to 16

Strawberry Crunch Cake

1   Combine and mix well (it is quite thick)
        2 c. flour
        2 T. whole wheat flour
        4 t. baking powder
        ½ c. sugar
        ¾ t. salt
        ¾ c. milk
        2 eggs
        ½ t. lemon extract
        1 t. vanilla.

2   Spread in a greased 10″ springform pan.

3   Sprinkle over top of batter
        2 c. fresh sliced strawberries
        ½ c. sugar.

4   In another bowl, mix with a fork until crumbly and sprinkle over strawberries
        ⅓ c. sugar
        ⅓ c. flour
        2 T. whole wheat flour
        ⅓ c. soft butter
        ¼ t. nutmeg.

5   Bake at 425° 30 to 40 minutes.

6   Serve warm with whipped cream.

Serves 10 to 12

German Chocolate Cake

1   Cream well
>   1 c. soft butter
>   2 c. sugar
>   ½ c. cocoa powder
>   1 t. vanilla
>   1 t. coconut extract.
2   Add one at a time and cream well after each
>   4 eggs.
3   In another bowl combine
>   2½ c. flour
>   ½ t. salt
>   2½ t. baking powder
>   ¼ t. baking soda.
4   Add flour mixture to butter mixture alternately with
>   1⅓ c. milk.
5   Blend well and pour into greased and floured 9" pans.
6   Bake at 350° 35 to 40 minutes or until top springs back to the touch.
7   Cool on rack for 10 minutes. Remove from pans and cool to room temperature.

Topping

8   Blend well
>   ½ c. brown sugar
>   ¼ c. melted butter
>   ½ t. vanilla
>   ¼ t. coconut extract
>   1 c. finely shredded coconut
>   ½ c. finely chopped pecans
>   2 T. light cream.

9   Spread topping on top layer and broil until browned. Cool before assembling cake.

10   Frost sides and middle with whipped butter frosting* with 1 square unsweetened chocolate (melted and cooled) and 1 t. coconut extract added.

See Whipped Butter Frosting recipe (page 149)
Serves 16

Tollhouse Cake

1   Cream well in a large bowl
>   1 c. soft butter
>   2 c. sugar.

2   Add one at a time, blending well after each addition
>   4 eggs
>   1 T. vanilla.

3   In another bowl combine
>   2 c. flour
>   ½ c. whole wheat flour (or use all white flour)
>   ½ t. salt
>   2½ t. baking powder.

4   Add flour mixture to egg mixture alternately with
>   1⅓ c. light cream or milk.

5   Blend until well mixed, then stir in
>   ½ c. chocolate chips
>   ½ c. chopped walnuts.

6   Pour in 2 greased and floured 9″ springform pans and bake at 350° 30 minutes or until top springs back.

7   Cool 15 minutes. Remove from pans and chill.

8   Frost with fudge frosting* and sprinkle with chopped walnuts.

See Fudge Frosting recipe (page 149)
Serves 12 to 16

Poppy Seed Cake

1   Mix together in a saucepan
        1½ c. milk
        1 c. poppy seeds.

2   Heat just to boiling and remove to refrigerator to cool for 30 minutes.

3   Cream at high speed until very fluffy
        1 c. soft butter
        1½ c. brown sugar
        1 t. vanilla.

4   Add one at a time and continue beating on high speed
        4 egg yolks.

5   Combine in another bowl
        2 c. flour
        2½ t. baking powder
        ¼ t. baking soda
        ½ t. salt.

6   Add dry ingredients to butter and sugar mixture alternately with milk mixture and blend well.

7   In a separate bowl, beat until stiff and fold into batter
        4 egg whites.

8   Pour in well greased and floured 9″ springform pans and bake at 350° for 50 minutes or until done and toothpick comes out clean.

9   Remove to rack to cool for 10 minutes. Remove from pans. Cut each layer in half horizontally and spread bottoms with apricot jam. Reassemble and frost with whipped butter frosting.* Sprinkle top with poppy seeds and chill until frosting hardens.

*See Whipped Butter Frosting recipe (page 149)
Serves 12 to 16

Fudge Marble Cake

1   Cream in a medium bowl
        1 c. soft butter
        2 c. sugar
        2 t. vanilla.

2   Add one at a time, blending well after each addition,
        4 egg yolks.

3   Combine in another bowl
        2½ c. flour
        2½ t. baking powder
        ½ t. salt
        ½ t. soda.

4   Add dry ingredients to butter and egg mixture alternately with
        1 c. buttermilk.

5   In another bowl, whip until stiff and fold in
        4 egg whites.

6   Divide batter in half. To one half add
        2 squares unsweetened chocolate, melted and cooled
        ½ t. nutmeg.

7   Alternating chocolate and yellow batters, drop by large spoonfuls into greased and floured 9″ pans (6 or 7 dollops in a circle) and swirl with a knife to create a marble effect. Do not overmix or marbling will disappear.

8   Bake at 350° for 30 to 35 minutes until top springs back when touched. Cool and frost with fudge frosting.*

*See Fudge Frosting recipe (page 149)
Serves 12 to 16

Butter Pecan Cake

1   Combine

        1 c. finely chopped pecans

        1 T. melted butter

2   Bake at 350° for 10 minutes until brown, then set aside to cool.

3   Cream well in a large bowl

        1 c. soft butter

        2 c. sugar.

4   Add one at a time and blend well after each addition

        4 eggs.

5   Blend in

        1 T. vanilla.

6   In another bowl combine

        2 c. flour

        ½ c. whole wheat flour (or use all white flour)

        ½ t. salt

        2½ t. baking powder.

7   Add flour mixture alternately with

        1⅓ c. light cream or milk.

8   Mix at medium speed until blended.

9   Reserve 2 T. of the pecans for the top of the cake. Stir the remaining pecans into the batter.

10   Pour into two greased and floured 9″ springform pans. Bake at 350° for 30 minutes or until the top springs back to the touch.

11   Cool 15 minutes. Remove from pans and chill.

12   Frost with whipped butter frosting* and decorate with the reserved 2 T. pecans. Chill.

*See Whipped Butter Frosting recipe (page 149)
Serves 16

Cappuccino Cake

1   Cream well in a large bowl
>   1 c. soft butter
>   2 c. sugar.

2   Add one at a time, blending well each time,
>   4 eggs
>   2 t. vanilla.

3   In another bowl combine
>   2 c. flour
>   ½ c. whole wheat flour (or use all white flour)
>   ½ t. salt
>   2½ t. baking powder
>   ¼ t. cinnamon.

4   Combine in a measuring cup, stirring to dissolve coffee,
>   1⅓ c. milk
>   2 T. instant coffee.

5   Add milk mixture to egg and sugar mixture alternately with flour mixture.

6   Grate medium fine
>   4 squares unsweetened chocolate.

7   Reserve ¼ c. grated chocolate. Stir remaining chocolate into cake batter.

8   Pour in greased and floured 9" springform pans. Bake at 350° 30 minutes or until top springs back.

9   Cool 15 minutes. Remove from pans and chill.

10   Frost with whipped butter frosting* 2 T. instant coffee, and ¼ t. cinnamon added to warm milk. Fold ¼ c. grated chocolate into frosting or sprinkle over frosting.

*See Whipped Butter Frosting recipe (page 149)
Serves 12 to 16

Orange Rum Cake

1   Puree in food processor or blender, then set aside:
      peel of 2 oranges
      peel of 1 lemon
      ¾ c. water.

2   Puree in blender or food processor, then strain into a saucepan and set aside;
      2 peeled oranges
      1 peeled lemon.

3   Cream well in a mixing bowl
      1 c. soft butter
      1 c. sugar.

4   Add one at a time, beating well after each,
      4 eggs.

5   Beat in until well combined
      1 c. heavy cream
      pureed orange and lemon peelings.

6   Combine in another bowl
      2¾ c. flour
      1 T. baking powder
      1½ t. baking soda.

7   Add flour mixture to sugar and egg mixture. Blend well.

8   Spoon into well greased and floured small Bundt type pan.

9   Bake at 350° for 45 minutes. Cool on a rack for 10 minutes.

10 Pour over cake
      ½ c. dark rum.

11 Turn out on to another rack and cool to room temperature.

12 Combine in a saucepan with orange and lemon juice that has been set aside
      ½ c. white sugar
      ½ c. brown sugar

13   Heat until sugar dissolves, then pour over cake (put a pan under the rack) 2 or 3 times to glaze.

14   Serve warm with whipped cream and sprinkle with nutmeg.

Serves 14 to 16

Banana Brandy Cake

1   Mix until thick and lemon colored

    3 eggs

    1¼ c. sugar.

2   Add and beat until thick and light yellow

    ½ c. melted and cooled butter

    1 t. vanilla.

3   Combine in another bowl

    2 c. flour

    ½ c. whole wheat flour (or use all white flour)

    ½ t. salt

    1 t. coriander or nutmeg

    2½ t. baking power

    ½ t. baking soda.

4   Add flour mixture to egg mixture alternately with

    1 c. pureed bananas

    2 T. brandy

    1¼ c. buttermilk.

5   Pour in greased and floured 9″ springform pans and bake at 350° 30 minutes or until top springs back.

6   Cool 15 minutes. Remove from pan and chill.

7   Frost with whipped butter frosting* (use 2 T. brandy in place of vanilla and add ½ t. coriander or nutmeg to frosting).

*See Whipped Butter Frosting recipe (page 149)
Serves 12 to 16

Fresh Apple Ginger Cake

1   Combine in a saucepan
    4 c. peeled and cored apples
    ¼ c. molasses
    2 T. applejack or ginger brandy.

2   Simmer until apples are soft enough to mash. Mash until smooth and set aside to cool.

3   Combine in a large mixing bowl
    1 c. melted butter
    1 c. molasses
    ½ c. sugar
    3 eggs
    1 t. vanilla
    ¼ c. applejack or ginger brandy.

4   In another bowl combine
    2 c. flour
    1 c. whole wheat flour
    ¼ t. salt
    ½ t. cinnamon
    ½ t. nutmeg
    ½ t. cloves
    1 t. ginger
    2 t. baking soda
    ½ t. baking powder.

5   Add dry ingredients to butter mixture alternately with
    1 c. hot apple juice or cider.

6   Stir in gently
    2 c. thinly sliced apples
    ½ c. chopped walnuts
    ½ c. raisins (optional).

7   Spread into 2 buttered and floured 9" pans. Bake at 350° for 45 minutes or until the top springs back when touched.

8   Cool layers to room temperature.

9   Cut layers in half and spread each with ⅓ of applesauce. Cut off top of one layer (for bottom layer of finished cake) and spread cut top with applesauce. Assemble cake layers. Frost with sweetened whipped cream and decorate with walnuts.

Serves 8 to 10

Cream Cake

1   In a large mixing bowl, whip until thickened, but not stiff
         2 c. heavy cream

2   Fold in carefully with a rubber spatula
         2 c. sifted granulated sugar.

3   Blend together then fold in
         4 eggs
         1 T. vanilla.

4   Sift together twice, then fold in carefully
         2½ c. flour
         ½ c. whole wheat flour (or use all white flour)
         4 t. baking powder
         ½ t. salt.

5   Only mix until all patches of white are incorporated.

6   Pour into 2 9" springform pans that have been buttered and sprinkled with granulated sugar.

7   Bake at 350° 30 minutes or until top springs back to the touch.

8   Cool 15 minutes. Remove from pans and chill.

This cake is very good and versatile. I like to cut the layers in half horizontally and spread the bottoms with apricot or raspberry jam and reassemble and frost with sweetened whipped cream or whipped butter frosting and decorate with fresh fruit.

Serves 12 to 16

Peach Kugen Cake

Topping

1   Mix until crumbly with a fork or pastry blender

         ⅓ c. flour

         ⅓ c. oatmeal

         ¼ c. brown sugar

         2 T. melted butter

         ⅛ t. nutmeg

         2 T. chopped pecans or walnuts.

2   Set aside while preparing custard.

Custard

3   Combine in a mixing bowl

         2 c. sour cream

         1 egg

         2 egg yolks

         ½ c. sugar

         1 t. vanilla

         ⅛ nutmeg.

4   Set aside while preparing cake.

Cake

5   Cream together in a mixing bowl

         ½ c. soft butter

         ½ c. sugar.

6   Add and blend well

         1 egg

         1 t. vanilla.

7   Combine in another bowl
        1¼ c. flour
        ¼ c. whole wheat flour
        1½ t. baking powder
        ⅛ t. baking soda
        ⅛ t. nutmeg.

8   Add flour mixture to egg mixture with
        ½ c. sour cream
        2 T. milk.

9   Spread cake in one 9″ greased springform pan.

10   Spread evenly over cake
        1½ to 2 c. sliced peaches

11   Pour custard over peaches.

12   Sprinkle topping over custard.

13   Bake at 350° 50 to 60 minutes. Turn off oven and leave cake in oven 30 minutes. Serve warm with whipped cream.

Serves 10

Piña Colada Cake

1   Cream well
        2 c. sugar
        1 c. soft butter.

2   Add one at a time and blend well
        4 eggs.

3   In another bowl, combine
        1 c. pineapple juice (unsweetened)
        ½ c. Coco Lopez coconut cream
        1 t. coconut extract
        1 T. rum.

4   Add pineapple juice mixture to sugar and eggs alternately with
        3 c. flour
        3 t. baking powder
        1 t. salt.

5   Mix well. Pour into 2 9" springform pans and bake at 350° for 35 to 45 minutes or until top springs back when touched.

6   Cool 15 minutes. Remove from pan and chill on rack.

Filling

7   Combine in a small pan and let stand 5 minutes
        ½ c. pineapple juice
        1 T. gelatin.

8   Heat to dissolve gelatin.

9   Puree until smooth in a blender
        2 c. crushed pineapple (unsweetened)
        1 T. rum
        pineapple juice and gelatin mixture.

10   Pour into a bowl and chill until half set.

11   In another bowl, whip until stiff
            1½ c. heavy cream
            ½ c. powdered sugar (sifted)
            1 T. rum
            1 t. coconut extract.
12   Fold half of whipped cream into pineapple mixture.

13   Cut each layer in half horizontally. Spread bottoms with pineapple or apricot jam and put back together.
14   Spread half of filling on 1 layer (cut off any roundness on the layers so they are flat). Put other layer on top and spread on remaining filling.
15   Frost sides with reserved whipped cream and decorate with pastry bag.
16   Sprinkle with coconut and chill well.

Serves 12 to 16

Chocolate Fudge Cake

1   Melt and cool to room temperature
>> ½ c. butter
>> 3 squares unsweetened chocolate.

2   Combine in a medium bowl
>> 3 eggs
>> 2¼ c. brown sugar
>> ¼ c. cocoa powder
>> 2 t. vanilla.

3   Blend in chocolate mixture.

4   Sift in another bowl
>> 2¼ c. flour
>> 2 t. baking soda
>> ½ t. salt.

5   Add dry ingredients to chocolate mixture alternately with
>> 1 c. sour cream
>> 1 c. boiling water (or coffee).

6   Pour in greased and floured 9″ pans.

7   Bake at 350° degrees 25 to 30 minutes.

8   Cool well and frost with fudge frosting.*

Serves 12 to 16

Peanut Fudge Cake

Use hot water not coffee and stir in ½ c. finely chopped peanuts to batter. Frost with peanut fudge frosting.*

Strawberry Fudge Cake

Make ½ the recipe. Cut the cooled cake in half and spread with strawberry jam. Make ½ recipe fudge frosting adding 2 T. strawberry liqueur instead of vanilla. Frost cake and decorate with whipped cream and fresh strawberries.

*See Fudge Frosting recipe (page 149)

Fudge Frosting

1   Melt together, then cool to room temperature
        4 squares unsweetened chocolate
        ½ c. butter.
2   Combine in mixing bowl
        4 c. powdered sugar
        ½ c. heavy cream or evaporated milk
        2 t. vanilla.
3   Add chocolate mixture gradually and whip on high speed until
     spreading consistency. Add more heavy cream if too thick. If
     frosting is too thin, place over ice and stir until thick.

Variations
Add ½ c. peanut butter and ¼ c. finely chopped peanuts for Peanut
Fudge Frosting.

Whipped Butter Frosting

1   Whip until light on high speed in medium bowl
        1 c. soft butter
        1 c. sugar.
2   Continuing on high speed, slowly add
        ⅔ c. warm (not hot) cream or milk
        2 t. vanilla.
3   Whip at least 5 minutes or until the consistency of whipped
     cream.
This is enough to frost one 9″ layer cake. It hardens up nicely when
cold. Let chill before cutting cake.

Variations
Coffee Frosting. Add 1 to 2 T. instant coffee to milk.
Chocolate Frosting. Add 1 square unsweeted chocolate melted and
cooled.

To Cook Crepes

1 Lightly oil an 8″ crepe pan and heat over medium flame until water beads and disappears immediately on surface.
2 Quickly pour a scant ¼ c. of batter into pan, turning the pan in a circular motion quickly to cover the bottom.
3 Cook until crepe loses wet appearance and is lightly browned on underside.
4 Loosen sides of crepe with a rubber spatula, then turn and brown lightly on other side.
5 Remove from pan onto paper towels and cool until ready to fill.

Peach Melba Crepes

1 Slice, combine, and set aside for 15 minutes
       6 to 8 c. fresh sliced peaches
       ½ c. sugar
       1 T. vanilla.
2 Cook dessert crepes* and set aside.
3 Spread cooled crepes with raspberry jam.
4 Whip until stiff
       3 c. heavy cream
       ⅓ c. powdered sugar.
5 Drain peaches and add juice to whipped cream, beating until stiff.
6 Reserve 2 c. whipped cream for garnish.
7 Spread remaining cream evenly onto crepes. Arrange peaches evenly on crepes and roll up. Serve two on a plate. Garnish with reserved whipped cream and slices of peaches or fresh raspberries. Sprinkle lightly with nutmeg.

*See Dessert Crepes recipe (next page)

Variations

1   Use apricot jam and fresh strawberries instead of peaches.
2   Black Forest Crepes. Use chocolate crepes* instead of dessert
      crepes with strawberry jam and fresh strawberries or cherries.

See Chocolate Crepes recipe (page 152)
Makes 28 crepes, which serves 12 to 14.

Dessert Crepes

1   Mix in blender until smooth
            1 egg
            2 egg yolks
            ⅔ c. milk
            ⅔ c. water
            ⅓ c. melted butter or oil
            ¼ c. Brandy
            1 c. white flour
            2 to 4 T. sugar
            1 t. grated lemon or orange peel.
2   Let batter stand 30 minutes before cooking.

Chocolate Crepes

1   Mix well in blender

        4 eggs

        1 c. light cream

        2 T. brandy or Amaretto

        ¾ c. water

        ⅓ c. cocoa powder

        ¼ c. melted butter

        ¾ c. white flour

        ¼ t. salt

        ¼ c. sugar

        1 t. vanilla.

2   Let batter stand 30 minutes before cooking.

Coeur à la Crème

1   Whisk in a saucepan

        1 c. sour cream

        1 c. heavy cream

        ½ c. sugar.

2   Heat over low heat.

3   Combine, let stand 5 minutes, then stir into warm mixture until gelatin dissolves

        2 t. gelatin

        ¼ c. strawberry or pineapple juice.

4   In a mixing bowl beat until soft and smooth

        8 oz. cream cheese.

5 Stir cream mixture in gradually to avoid lumps.

6 Beat until smooth, then add
    ½ t. vanilla
    ¼ t. lemon or orange extract.

7 Pour into lightly oiled heart molds. Chill, unmold and garnish with strawberries or layer in parfait glasses with fresh or frozen fruits (strawberries, pineapple, blueberries, etc.) Chill well before serving.

Serves 8

Vanilla Custard

1 Mix in top of double boiler
    ¾ c. sugar
    2 T. cornstarch
    2 c. light cream or milk
    3 egg yolks and 1 egg
    dash salt.

2 Cook over boiling water until thick, whisking frequently.

3 Remove from heat and stir in
    1 t. vanilla.

4 Cool to room temperature.

5 Whip until stiff and fold into custard.
    1½ c. heavy cream.

This is very good over fresh fruit in a parfait glass or with 1 T. Amaretto added and poured over peaches and garnished with toasted almonds.

Chocolate Custard

Add ¼ to ½ c. cocoa to recipe above.

Trifle

Cake

1   Beat until light and thick
             2 eggs
             1 c. sugar
             1 t. vanilla or almond extract.
2   Heat to melt butter and blend into egg mixture gradually
             ½ c. light cream or milk
             1 T. butter.
3   Combine and stir into above until just mixed
             1 c. flour
             ¼ t. salt
             1 t. baking powder.
4   Pour into 9″ pan buttered and floured.
5   Bake at 350° for 25 minutes. Cool.

Custard

6   Combine in top of double boiler in order given
             1½ c. sugar
             ¼ c. cornstarch
             dash salt
             4 c. light cream
             ⅓ c. (8) egg yolks.
7   Cook over boiling water, stirring often until thick. Cool to
     room temperature.
8   Stir in
             1 T. vanilla (or 1 t. vanilla and 1 t. almond extract).
9   Cool to room temperature.
10   Whip until stiff, then fold in
             1 c. heavy cream

11   Cut cake into cubes 1½" square and fill parfait glasses half full
      of cake.

12   Sprinkle over cake in each glass
                1 to 2 T. sweet sherry or rum.

13   Melt in a double boiler
                1½ c. raspberry or peach jam.

14   Spoon jam evenly over cake.

15   Divide evenly over jam
                3 to 4 c. assorted fresh fruits (peaches, cherries, strawber-
                ries, etc.)

16   Divide custard evenly over fruit.

17   Garnish with toasted almonds.

Serves 10 to 15

For Chocolate Trifle

1   Add 1 square melted unsweetened chocolate to step 2.

2   Add ⅓ c. cocoa powder to custard.

3   Use rum instead of sherry when assembling.

4   Use raspberry or cherry jam.

5   Use canned dark cherries or fresh raspberries or strawberries for
     fruit.

6   Garnish with sweetened whipped cream.

Fresh Strawberry Mousse

1   Combine in a bowl
        4 c. sliced fresh strawberries
        ½ c. powdered sugar
        1 T. Triple Sec.
2   Let stand 15 to 20 minutes to release juice. Strain, reserving all juice.
3   Puree strawberries in a blender until smooth.
4   To reserved juice add
        1½ T. gelatin.
5   Let stand 5 minutes to soften gelatin, then heat in a small saucepan to dissolve gelatin.
6   Add gelatin to pureed strawberries in a bowl and mix well to incorporate gelatin.
7   Chill until mixture begins to set, but is not stiff.
8   In another bowl beat until stiff
        1½ c. heavy cream.
9   Reserve 1 c. for garnish and fold remainder into strawberry mixture.
10 Pour mousse into dishes and chill well.
11 Garnish with reserved whipped cream and a strawberry.

This is also good layered with chocolate mousse and topped with whipped cream flavored with vanilla and garnished with fresh strawberries, or served over sliced peaches, or used as a filling for cream cake.*

*See Cream Cake recipe (page 143)
Makes 1 pie or 8 to 10 parfaits.

Vanilla or Butterscotch Mousse

1   Mix well
        1 c. light cream
        3 egg yolks
        ¾ c. sugar
        1 T. gelatin softened in ¼ c. cold water.
2   Cook in top of double boiler until mixture is thick and coats a
    metal spoon.
3   Add and cool to room temperatuare
        1 T. vanilla.
4   Whip until stiff and fold in
        1 c. heavy cream.
5   Whip until stiff and fold in
        3 egg whites.
6   Stir in
        ½ c. chopped nuts.
7   Pour into mousse cups or parfait glasses alone or with fresh
    fruits or nuts or pour in cooked and cooled graham cracker crust
    and chill well.
8   Garnish with sweetened whipped cream, if desired.

Butterscotch Mousse

Use brown sugar and add 2 T. Brandy with vanilla.

*See Graham Cracker Crust recipe (page 106)
Serves 8

Rum n' Cider Mousse

1   Combine and let stand 5 minutes
  ¼ c. Cider
  2 T. gelatin.
2   Heat to dissolve gelatin and add to
  ¾ c. cider
  1 c. rum
  1 c. maple syrup
  1 t. vanilla.
3   Chill until half set.
4   Whip until stiff. Reserve 1½ c. for garnish and fold in remainder to cider mixture
  4 c. whipping cream
  ¼ t. nutmeg.
5   To reserved cream add and whisk until stiff
  2 T. powdered sugar or maple syrup
  1 t. vanilla.
6   Pour rum and cider mixture in dishes and chill well.
7   Garnish with reserved cream and sprinkle with nutmeg.

Serves 8 to 10

Pumpkin Nut Mousse

1   Combine and let stand 5 minutes
     ½ c. water
     1 T. gelatin.

2   Heat to dissolve gelatin.

3   Mix together until smooth
     ¾ c. maple syrup
     1 16-oz. can pumpkin
     1 t. vanilla
     1 T. brandy.

4   Blend in gelatin until well mixed and chill until half set.

5   Whip until stiff and fold in
     2 c. whipping cream.

6   Blend in
     ½ c. chopped walnuts or pecans.

7   Pour into dishes and chill well. For a pie, pour into a baked
     and cooled graham cracker crust.*

See Graham Cracker Crust recipe (page 106)
Serves 8 to 10

Cappuccino Mousse

1   Combine and let stand for 5 minutes

         ¼ c. water

         1 T. gelatin.

2   Combine with

         2 c. hot espresso

         ¼ c. sugar

         2 T. Creme de Cocoa

         ¼ t. vanilla.

4   Chill until half set.

5   Beat until stiff and fold in

         2 egg whites.

6   Whip until stiff

         1½ c. heavy cream

         3 T. powdered sugar

         ¼ t. vanilla

         dash cinnamon.

7   Set aside ½ c. whipped cream for garnish. Fold the remainder into the espresso mixture with

         ½ c. grated semisweet chocolate.

8   Pour into parfait glasses or mousse cups. Garnish with whipped cream, chocolate curls, and sprinkles of cinnamon. Can be poured into cooked and cooled graham cracker crust.* Chill well.

*See Graham Cracker Crust recipe (page 106)
Serves 8

Chocolate Rum Mousse

1   Heat over a low flame until sugar dissolves
         1½ c. sugar
         ¾ c. rum.
2   In another pan melt over low heat
         12 oz. unsweetened chocolate.
3   Combine chocolate and rum mixture in a large bowl and stir in
         ½ c. heavy cream.
4   Cool to room temperature.
5   Beat until stiff and fold in
         6 egg whites.
6   Beat until stiff and fold in
         3 c. heavy cream
         1 t. vanilla.
7   Spoon into mousse cups and chill.
8   Garnish with additional sweetened whipped cream and
     chocolate curls.

Serves 12 to 15

Piña Colada Parfait

1   Have on hand
        3 c. unsweetened pineapple juice.
2   Pour ½ c. unsweetened pineapple juice in a saucepan, add
        2 T. gelatin.
3   Let stand 5 minutes to soften.
4   Heat to dissolve, then add and stir until dissolved
        ½ c. sugar.
5   Add gelatin mixture to 2½ c. unsweetened pineapple juice in a
    bowl with
        ½ c. Coco Lopez coconut cream
        ¼ c. dark rum.
6   Blend well, then remove half of mixture to a measuring cup
    and set the rest in the refrigerator.
7   Divide the mixture in the measuring cup evenly among 6 to 8
    parfait glasses and set them in the refrigerator.
8   When mixture is fairly stiff, evenly distribute over it
        ½ c. crushed drained pineapple.
9   Refrigerate again.
10 When mixture in bowl is partially set, but not stiff, whip until
    stiff in another bowl
        1 c. heavy cream.
11 Fold half of whipped cream into gelatin mixture and divide
    evenly over pineapple in parfait glasses.
12 Sprinkle evenly over each
        ½ c. sweetened coconut.
13 To reserved whipped cream, add and beat until stiff
        1 T. rum
        1 t. coconut extract
        2 T. powdered sugar.
14 Garnish parfaits with the sweetened whipped cream and top
    with a strawberry or cherry.

Serves 6 to 8

Key West Fruit Parfait

1   Slice into a bowl
         4 c. peaches or strawberries.
2   Add and mix well
         ½ c. sugar
         ½ t. lemon extract
         2 T. peach or strawberry brandy.
3   Let stand while preparing pudding.
4   Combine in a small pan and let stand 5 minutes
         ⅓ c. lemon juice
         1 t. gelatin.
5   Heat to dissolve gelatin.
6   In another bowl mix well
         1 can condensed milk
         4 egg yolks
         lemon and gelatin mixture.
7   In a separate bowl whip until stiff
         2 c. heavy cream.
8   Reserve 2 c. of whipped cream and fold remainder into lemon
     and egg mixture.
9   Divide fruit among 6 to 8 parfait glasses or glass bowls.
     Distribute any juice left in bowl evenly over fruit.
10   Divide pudding evenly over the fruit.
11   To reserved whipped cream add and mix in until cream is thick
         2 T. sifted powdered sugar
         1 T. peach or strawberry brandy.
12   Garnish pudding with flavored whipped cream and a slice of
     peach or strawberry.

Serves 6 to 8

Index

About the Authors

Shirley Edes lives with her husband, Steve, and their daughter, Betsy, in a 200-year-old cape in a state of perpetual remodeling in the remote town of Goshen, New Hampshire. She surrounds herself with flowers, raspberries, and dogs with an inordinate interest in porcupines.

She moonlighted in many local kitchens while working on a college degree, which proved less satisfying than cooking. After four years at Peter Christian's, she is still smiling at the soup counter, but she still dreams of a country inn in her dotage.

Julia Philipson lives in Cilleyville, New Hampshire, with an ever-changing array of chickens, sheep, pigs, dogs, cats, and parakeets. She has been baking, creating, and gaining weight at Peter Christian's for five and a half years while trying to keep the flowers, vegetables, magazines, comic books, junk collections (and her figure) under reasonable control — with occasional success.

After seven years of art schools — from Cleveland to New York — she gradually decided to put her creativity into cooking rather than drawing; the creative ideas for new ways to prepare food keep on coming, the results are more immediate (and the pay is better).

Murray Washburn lives in Etna, New Hampshire, with his wife, Karen, and their four children — Murray, Peter, Wynne, and Anne — and a sometimes exasperating menagerie of animals. Karen carpenters on their solar home and artfully executes complex catering jobs, while Murray rides herd over three Peter Christian's Taverns.

The two founded the original "PC's" in 1973 as a quiet family-and-friends effort, with carved wooden booths and tables, stoneware crocks and plates, and with a deliberate emphasis on delicious food served in a setting that reflected "We care!" Little has altered over the past ten or so years save the "quiet" has been displaced by an audible buzz of loyalty and enthusiasm demonstrated by patrons and staff alike.